T0288520

Adirondack

FRENCH
LOUIE

Adirondack

French Louie

Early Life in the North Woods

by Harvey L. Dunham

Text Illustrations by Frank Devecis

Chapter Headings by the Author

Over a Hundred Reproductions from Old Photographs

North Country Books
Utica, New York

ADIRONDACK
FRENCH LOUIE

ISBN-10 0-932052-57-6
ISBN-13 978-0-932052-57-5

NORTH COUNTRY BOOKS
220 Lafayette Street
Utica, New York 13502

To Davy

The old creek flows on, the
sun shines, the birds sing and
the best pools to fish are ahead of you.

"I called on the king. . . .
There was a man in my neighborhood
who lived in a hollow tree. . . .
I should have done better
had I called on him."

THOREAU

A Look Back

For we can not remain and we can not return,

We must follow old time in his track;

But the campfires of old in our memory burn—

*And we stop and we take a look back.**

AN OLD MAN said, "I knew French Louie."

Another . . . and another old timer told his tale. And these recollections have been woven together in this story of the lower Adirondacks just as they recalled it.

It is not a story of the achievement of great fame or riches, nor has it the hell and high-water flavor of romantic adventure in the Great West. It's merely a homely narrative about a remarkable old character in his way and the simple life in our own "North Woods" before and at the turn of the century.

Old George Wandover was back in the woods when I stopped at his small weather beaten house in Wheelertown. I waited for

*From TOTE-ROAD AND TRAIL, by Douglas Malloch, copyright 1917, 1945, used by special permission of the publishers, The Bobbs-Merrill Company, Inc.

him, sitting on a time-worn wagon-box, and in about an hour or so he came in, a tall, lanky, honest, taciturn pioneer with creased leathery face and hands. He had a six quart pail full of blueberries, "big and juicy and sweet from great big bushes on the edge of the woods."

He was one who said, "Yes, I knew French Louie."

We drove ten miles through flat wooded country to Buffalo Head to see Byron Cool. Byron came out of his house, took one look at George in the car, turned and hollered for his wife.

"Ma. Come out here. Look it. Look it what they got caged up here." They had a great time going back over the old trails together.

In a board and tar-papered shack within a stone's throw of the West Canada Creek in Wilmurt I found an old fellow named Paul Hoppe. He swore, got up and paced around the room on the uneven floor, sat down and looked me right in the eye and then, with both his fists, knocked his own head. He was mad because he could not remember.

"Oh Boy!" he yelled. And like a victrola running down, "Oh Boy, Oh boy, oh boy," until he was quiet again and stared at me in the dim light of fading day. From outside the shack came the steady low roar of the old West Creek.

"I useter ride dem log," Paul said softly. Then he raised his voice. "There was no driver on the whole West Crick could ride dem log better 'n Paul Hoppe. I went out to get some wood today. A maple blew down out back here 'n I was goin' to work me up a little wood. I got me up there two feet off the ground and I'm a son-of-a-gun, I was dizzy. I useter ride dem log in moccasins an' ba jeez, I was dizzy! French Louie? Sure, I knew French Louie."

Another old fellow was sitting on his porch dragging on a pipeful of "Warnicky Brown." His wife was there and she shouted at him, "Bill, you knew Louie. French Louie." Old Bill Clark smiled. His face beamed and he sat up straight with his shoulders back and looked at me but he did not say a word.

"Yes," his wife said, "he knew French Louie but he can't talk. He had a stroke and he can't talk."

Then there was one who did not want to remember. He had been a hotel keeper in the little town of Speculator and had taken a good many thousand dollars worth of furs from French Louie. His conscience must have been bothering him for he answered me: "Never heard of 'im! Never heard of 'im!"

But Isaac Kenwell, of Indian Lake, at ninety-five, who had known Louie for forty-five years, and Wellington Kenwell, and "Pants" Lawrence, and Jim Sturges, who as a boy had trapped with Louie, all recalled much. And there was Truman Haskell and Eddie Robertson of Barneveld, guide Jim Wadsworth and Lumberman Sol Carnahan and Hotel Man Bill Wright, all of whom had known Louie and had known the old West Creek. All good woodsmen, they and many others told and relived their experiences and gave us this true picture. Nor can you blame them if in their fading memories certain scenes and happenings became somewhat confused.

As for the lore of the lumberjacks . . . when the bartender at the Union Hotel in Prospect was asked, "Is there an old tote-teamster around town by the name of Johnny McCullen?", his chin dropped as he leaned forward over the bar to steady himself.

"Why he . . . why Johnny's been dead for . . . for twenty-five years."

"How about Mel Paul?"

"Say," he said, as the idea of what I was after finally dawned on him, "the fellow you want to see is Trume Brown, second house from the corner, Lumberjack. He can tell you all about them days."

Trume Brown was home. A solid man with both feet on the ground. In his kitchen, that night, he drove the river and broke the jams again. Johnny McCullen was there, and Sol and Ab Carnahan, Jim Hill and Gene McBeth; all of them were with us around the little kitchen stove that cold winter night. Trume sure had his calks on, his long peavey in hand as he recalled the old times and their perils. Ab Carnahan was drowned again that night.

And so we, who love the Adirondacks, and especially that lower section where the West Canada Creek takes its rise, are deeply thankful to all those old timers. We must also acknowledge our indebtedness to yellowed copies of "Forest and Stream," "Forest Leaves" and other now quaint publications, for this glimpse of woods life just before and after 1900.

There are indeed places in this book, such as the section about lumbering and the one about Barber's Place on Jocks Lake, where the trail of the old hunter and trapper runs a little dim. These, however, are part of history too—glimpses of the Great North Woods at the very time French Louie was busy at becoming an almost legendary character. And for that matter, he even played an humble role in the lumbering operations while occasionally he strayed as far west as Jocks Lake.

French Louie! Every neck of the woods had its French Louie, each well known in his immediate locality. The Fulton Chain region had a French Louie at Rondax Lake, the Morehouseville section had one; at Tupper Lake Junction a French Louie "lived in a log cabin and froze to death in a snow bank with a St. Regis Squaw;" there was one at Northville and there was a French Louie around Cranberry Lake. The woods were full of them; but the greatest of them all, known from Boonville to North Creek, was French Louie of the West Canada Lakes.

They were all typical, a product of the times. Originally trappers, they settled in the forest on state lands or lands of the lumber companies; as squatters they built their cabins and lived off the country. They hunted and fished; they trapped and picked spruce gum and made maple sugar, trading the furs and these other products at the settlements for supplies. They sought seclusion, but hunters and fishermen from the outside world found them out and used their cabins for shelter and their stoves and fireplaces to cook on. The intrusion made them mad, but they were glad to get the silver dollars and the presents they received. They soon found themselves guiding for the outsiders and running a place in the woods for fishing parties in the spring and for hunting parties in the fall.

The West Canada Lakes, where "the greatest of them all" abode, you may reach today by following up the West Canada Creek—"creek" by name but larger than many rivers—which flows into the Mohawk River at Herkimer, going first by car through farmlands into the beginning of the woods; then by tote road and trail, northward along a rocky stream, past wild black still-waters, and when the trail peters out, through tangled alders and leg-breaking windfalls. If you go on up the "Ol' Wes' Crick" far enough, to its headwaters, you come to the West Canada Lakes.

This was a neck o' the woods hardly known until its French Louie came into it. Early surveyors did not penetrate it. This is shown clearly in the Report of the Topographic Survey of the Adirondacks by Verplanck Colvin in 1873, who with his party explored no farther west than these lakes. But the trappers, they went everywhere, even in the earliest days. Famous pioneers of the trapline were Green White, Jock Wright, Nick Stoner and Nat Foster.

On North Lake, or Big West as it was called, is a clearing which has been the stopping place for hunters, trappers and woodsmen for over a hundred years. Redmen might have been the first to stop there, to cut a few trees on the lakeshore for building crude shelters and for their fires. As time went on, others followed—trappers and exploring woodsmen, later fishermen and sportsmen. The opening in the forest enlarged and one shelter replaced another. At any rate, sometime after 1850 the few hardy men whom trapping had taken so deep into the wilderness, told of signs in this clearing at the outlet of Big West which indicated that a small log camp had once stood there. It had all rotted and was gone, leaving only a faint trace of foundation logs. Then a few years later Chet Sturges and Marinus Lawrence, trappers from Newton's Corners,* a town to the southeast, built a slab shanty against the flat side of a large rock on the woods side of the clearing.

This shack became the home of French Louie, the last real woodsman to actually live in the clearing. A quiet, strong character, resourceful, fearless, peaceful in this seclusion, he could not sign his own name but if he had been able to, he would have signed it "Louis Seymour," and he lived there in the West Canada clearing for over thirty years, from the 70's until 1915.

---

* Now Speculator

Contents

Illustrations

Over the Mountains

Chapter One

It was a late Indian Summer day in the Fall of 1868 when French Louie first came to the North Woods. Some people long after remembered seeing him climb down from the buckboard stage at Indian Lake Village and stand in front of the Kenwell & Roblee store, working the kinks out of his joints after the long, jolting ride over the mountains from North Creek.

They saw a stockily built man, 36 years of age, not tall but deep chested, with broad shoulders, very long arms and strong hands, a large head with light curly hair and sparkling blue-black eyes, narrow but smiling, and a typical French Canadian moustache. The spirit of the Coureurs de bois was his heritage; the gay nature of the bon voyageur and the politeness of the habitant were his; all showing through a stoicism which must have come from a touch of Algonquin Indian, even with brown curly hair. He weighed about one hundred and sixty, looked as hard as Laurentian granite and as tough as Adirondack spruce.

He had been born on a small, newly cleared farm near Dog

River, north of Ottawa, Canada, in 1832. They had called him a calf because be was born in April. There in the backwoods he grew to be a strong boy, broad backed and solid, with hard muscular arms that moved things and hands that gripped like the traps he set in the bordering forest.

There was always plenty to do on that rough little place, always land to make, stumps to remove, alders and brush to chop or pull out. His mother and father, his many brothers and sisters worked hard, and Louie, when he was but a boy of eight, did almost a man's work. When his mother died, a stepmother took her place and things did not go so well. While working in the fields he thought of running away. One evening in late summer he received a smart cuff on the ear for sitting in his brother's chair at the supper table, and that night under cover of darkness, after lying low behind the woodshed until very late, he left home. And left his brief and struggling boyhood behind him. To him there was little else to leave; but on that cool northern night as he stumbled down the dark and stony road, he took the spirit of youth with him. It was fortunate that he had this spirit, for he needed it on the rough roads that lay ahead. Without even a bundle under his arm he went away, not into the woods which he knew so well, but south toward the city.

A circus was showing in a small town and Louie worked to see the performance and stayed to see three shows. When the circus pulled out, he left with it and stayed with it until it went into winter quarters.

That winter, in the city of Montreal, he slept in barrels and ate whatever was thrown out to him. A homeless, ragged, unwanted boy, he hung around the markets and the waterfront and worked some on the smaller boats. Soon he crossed over into the States and joined up with a circus, working nights and sleeping days. The people he was thrown in with were a tough lot, but Louie had a certain way about him so that he got along and could hold his own with any of them.

All talk was of the Erie Canal, although it had been open for more than fifteen years. The freighters and the bright packets were the admiration of all who saw them. Even the Irish diggers shared in the glory and swelled with pride over their part in the making. New lines were formed—more boats, more mules, more men.

As a boy of twelve Louie hired out as driver at eight dollars a month and found, followed the mules on the long tow-path, trudged mile upon mile in all kinds of weather, witnessed the many fights in the thick aired taverns along the route, fought and drank enough blackstrap to drown an ordinary boy. Some captains were hard. "De ol' man on dat string o' boats was wan awful ol' man," are Louie's words.

Yet it was not a bad job. Sometimes it was muddy and his feet were heavy, but anyway he was always on the move, going somewheres, outdoors, and there was plenty of wild country alongside the tow-path. On summer days, Louie, his keen eyes ever searching, picked out wild life that most drivers, trudging behind their mules, would have passed unnoticed. Deer on the border of woodlands, mink moving like a shadow along a log on the edge of a small stream, foxes turning in their trot on a hillside to take a look at the big canal boat, muskrats on some backwater; rabbits, squirrels or a soaring hawk or sleeping owl. Songbirds were there too, but Louie hardly knew that they were there. The grosbeak and the thrasher singing to all the world from the uppermost tree-tops, warblers and sparrows in the brush and swallows over the water; but Louie's eye and ear were tuned to bigger game. He dreamed. He picked out good places for trap sets, good places to build a cabin. Only a boy yet he itched to get his hands on a gun and go back into these wooded hills that looked down on him as he plodded along, singing softly to himself or to his old mule, Sal:

"De Erie, she's arisin',
An' de whiskey's gettin' low.
We don't get noder drink
'Till we get to Buffalo."

At the stopping places Louie, though never afraid, was not one to start trouble. He was no bully. The other boy drivers were

3

slow to pick a fight with him; for they knew his great strength and that he had a temper that would fly up at times as though he would as soon kill a man as look at him.

There was much "hollering" on the canal. The canalers always had to "holler" as they approached each lock along with the bugle of the steersman to warn the locktenders. And there were other occasions for such vocal displays. The canal for some distance west of Rome was laid through a swamp and at a place called the "Black Snake" because of certain bends in it just above Wood Creek aqueduct, "a lad twelve or thirteen years old was seized by a panther and dragged into the forest, the frightened horse he was driving jumping into the canal. For a long time after, so terror stricken were the young drivers from hearing this story, it was almost impossible to get any of them to drive through the swamp after dark, and many a boy ran off and left his team rather than chance it."* Along this "Black Snake" section or in other seemingly panther-infested areas, drivers would buck up their courage by challenging anything within hearing with their fearsome yells. Louie was a past master at it; and they envied his ability to make their hair stand on end with a terrible cry when their boats passed in the night. Many years later the quiet people of the Adirondack villages of Indian Lake, Speculator and Lake Pleasant were to hear long, blood-curdling yells, not unlike that of a panther or wolf, when Louie came out of the backwoods to satisfy the little that was gregarious in him.

Once Louie went back to Canada and found that his family had separated. He never saw them again. In a short time he was back again to the States, keeping much to himself, minding his own business, plodding along on his adventurous way.

For the next twenty years, until after the Civil War, Louie spent much of his life on the canals and with small circuses. When the canals were closed and the circuses were back in winter quarters, he worked in the woods, living the life of a lumberjack, and he became a master at hazardous river driving and clean chopping.

It was near the end of the season in 1868 that a circus that

* From Sims' "Frontiersman."

4

Louie was with was showing at Saratoga. Crews of lumberjacks had come into the town to see the freaks, the wax exhibits, the minstrels and to blow off steam generally. From them he heard enough about a great country to the north, back over the mountains, to make him want to go there, and when the circus left Saratoga, it was minus a tent man; its Louie Seymour was on the steam cars bound north on the Sacketts Harbor & Saratoga Railroad, which was then under construction and planning to cross the entire woods, past Blue Mountain and Racquette and by some route through the Big Moose and Beaver River country on to Carthage and Sacketts Harbor and to lumber some five hundred thousand acres of timber land.

Somewhere in the directions it went was this Indian Lake place that Louie had been hearing about.

He had said "Indian Lake" to the ticket seller and received a ticket to Thurman Station. The conductor on the cars told him, "From there take the stage to Warrensburg where you get another stage to North Creek."

After rattling along for about fifty miles, stopping and starting, the train finally arrived at Thurman Station and Louie grabbed his bundle and piled off.

"Warrensburg stage," the drivers were shouting.

"Indian Lake?" Louie asked one of them.

"Sure. Indian Lake. Get right up on there."

Louie got into the back seat of a fringed canopy-top spring seater. The wheezing engine and the confusion of a new railroad were left behind when the horses trotted off over the dusty road to Warrensburg. The North Creek stage wasn't in yet when he arrived there but it wasn't long before the bartender at the tavern said, "You goin' to North Creek?"

"Indian Lake," Louie said.

"Your stage is out there now." And again he was on his way.

After staying overnight in a hotel at North Creek, he took a seat in a long, high wheeled buckboard stage for the trip over the mountains. It was a full day's drive, mostly through dark spruce

5

and balsam forests, with slow creaking hauls up steep stony pitches and over pavement-like granite brows where the climb eased off; then down almost as slowly with braked buckboard, over narrow roads along the edges of precipitous drops, to smooth sandy stretches through grassy beaver meadows and clearings. The stage rattled across bridges over spruce-black North Woods water, toiled through oozing ruts past swamps with the forest closing in on either side except where there were clearings, some not more than choppings, with bark-roofed log houses, lean-to barns and shacks and small roughly fenced in gardens with the smell of woodsmoke and the sight of natives raising a hand in greeting from the doorways. At length, before the sun had set, the tired horses and the tired passengers came out into flat open country, one big clearing for miles, with towering ridges and peaks in the western distance. Where a few houses, of rude frame or log construction, huddled together, was their destination.

So Louis Seymour, French Canadian with a streak of Irish, but as he himself put it, "All Indian," came to Indian Lake village. He fitted right in with what he saw before him; woodsmen and lumberjacks and leather skinned tote-teamsters with their teams of big broad-backed horses, who had come into town from the backwoods camps to load up with tools and flour, beans, pork, oats, hay, for a long hard haul back through hub-deep mud and over rocks and holes and rough corduroy. As a backdrop stood the dark pointed firs of a balsam flat, silhouetted in the soft light of the late afternoon against mountains that were splotched with patches of green timber and hardwoods and steep rocky faces; mountains that beckoned one to come and see what lay beyond them.

This was what Louie was born for. In the clearing in Canada, encircled by primitive forest of birch against solid backgrounds of dense spruce, he had inherited and developed that French Canadian trait, a fondness for the "bush." Now it had cropped out in him in full force; and he was drinking in the scene, while working the kinks out of his joints after that hard ride, when a tall and wiry young native of the village went out of his way to speak to the newly arrived Canuck.

6

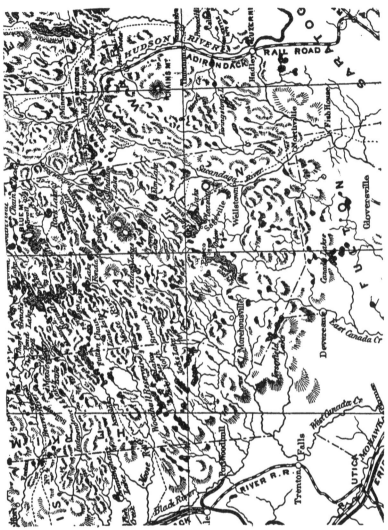

A SECTION OF COLVIN'S SURVEY MAP OF 1873

The next undertaking was the exploration of the sources of Cedar river, about which much doubt existed. On one map a chain of ponds, which I had long known as the Cedar lakes (and which I had supposed were at the head waters of Cedar river), are shown as part of the West Canada lakes or sources of the West Canada creek, flowing westward. On another map, at this moment commonly sold to travelers of the wilderness, it is shown emptying into Moose river, under the name of Moose lake. These I knew to be mistakes, but it was important to prove them so.

7

"Hello," he said, meeting Louie's squinting friendly eyes.

"Work?" Louie asked. "She plaintee?"

"Griffin's hirin' men. You want a job?"

"On de lumberwoods. Dees Greefin lumber camp. W'ere she be?"

The young fellow pointed toward a road going into the woods to the south.

"Follow that road," he said. "Follow it to Lewey Lake and tell 'em Ike Kenwell sent you."

Trapline to Indian Clearing

Chapter Two

"They're as wild a bunch of jacks as ever was seen,
And they all work for Griffin on Township Nineteen."

Louie followed the road south into the bare hardwoods, shuffling through the dry leaves, over rocks, around mud holes, alongside the deep wheel ruts, the road winding about to avoid bog holes or too much steepness. Partridges whirred off and squirrels scolded him. Nuthatches and woodpeckers and flocks of busy chickadees took no notice of him, but the flickers, gathering together before starting for warmer climates, kept flying up ahead of him on the road, and bluejays, clamoring, all excited, screamed alarm. He met and stepped aside for a toter who waved to him from his swaying wagon seat. He met a couple of lumberjacks. "B'jour, b'jour." He saw where much cordwood was being gotten out and felt that he must be nearing the camp. Soon there was the lake at the foot of a great mountain and the clearing and the long low log buildings. This was Griffin's camp, owned by George

Griffin, a big lumberman who had thirteen camps or shanties scattered about the woods in the Lewey Lake and Indian Lake sections.

That same day Louie was hired as a blacksmith's helper.

The blacksmith in a lumbercamp is a very important part of the outfit. Give a good man a hammer and a pair of tongs and he can make or fix anything. Grapples broken when skidding, chains to be gone over, toggles to be repaired, whiffletrees and neckyokes to be mended, dull calks to be replaced, great spikes to be cut and pointed for the building of the dams. The log rollers filed their hooks four or five times a day, until, when the points were all dubbed off, they took their peavies to the blacksmith to get new points. There was always something to build or something to be fixed, so Louie had plenty to do.

But Louie wanted to get out among the trees. He liked to chop. He enjoyed using a sharp well hung ax. It was not long before he went into the woods as a chopper, working with the one man who was at least as good as he, Dick Burch; and Dick must have been all right for he married his boss's daughter, Mary Griffin.

The logs were chopped, none cut under twelve inches on the stump. Arguments on sawing logs were just beginning to be heard. It was thought that a sawed log would split all up when they were being driven down the rivers, that logs had to be chopped so as to get the necessary tapered ends. Anyway, crosscut saws were scarce and costly; the ones in use had to be imported from England; and there were few men who knew how to sharpen one. Also in those days there were few double bitted axes.

Louie stayed with Griffin. In 1871 he worked a small lumber job for this operator on a tract at the lower end of Lewey Lake. For the job he bought a yoke of spotted oxen, and still had them two years later when he geed and hawed a load of hides through the town of Newton Corners, taking them to the tannery for Dave Sturges. Ten-year old Jim Sturges, Dave's nephew, strode manlike along beside Louie and the oxen, and Louie little knew of his own greatness and the deep and lasting impression that he was making on the boy's mind.

Between 1871 and '73 Louie worked in the lumberwoods for Jim MacCormack and John McGinn, and drove logs on the Jessup River for Dave Sturges. He was a good man on the drive.

Like most lumberjacks, Louie never held on very long to the money he made in the woods. He was a lone wolf, spending it for liquor and having a good time all by himself, harming no one. Isaac Kenwell did not forget him, and when he saw Louie in the settlements at these times, he tried to help him. There was something about Louie that people had to like.

"Why do you act the way you do?" Kenwell asked Louie, "wasting hundreds of dollars and getting nothing out of it, except tramping around the town in your socks or bare feet and yelling like a panther or a wolf?"

"Meester Kenwell, ah do sam ting lak white man do," Louie told him. He was pleased to think of himself as an Indian. In the settlements or at his work in the woods, he stayed within himself; he stood apart from all the others; he was different. He was not just another lumberjack. He was "Louie."

What he wanted more than anything else was to get far back into the woods where he could hunt and fish, run his trap lines, and build a cabin; free as a hawk, and not be bothered by the rules and repressions of lumber camps and settlements. He liked to build things out of whatever the wilderness had to offer, and throw up little temporary shelters wherever night found him. He wanted to be way back in the woods, "where there was no one to tell him to pick it up or lay it down."

In the fall of 1873, Louie gave up following lumber jobs, and on Lewey Lake, in the shadow of the Blue Ridge and towering Snowy Mountain, sometimes called Squaw's Bonnet, he built his first little enclosed camp. Here he lived and trapped and sold his furs at Indian Lake village through Oliver Ste. Marie, who now owned the Kenwell store. He had no steel traps but used snares and dead-falls. Oliver took the furs and sent them to Prouty in New York City, who paid the best for furs. Louie could not save money, yet it might be a year or two before these Oliver Checks would show up to be cashed.

11

During that winter he captured two deer, built a small pen, and fed the animals on shin hemlock, a diet of which the captives were very fond. Later the deer were sold to the owner of a park in Saratoga.

On the opposite shore of Lewey Lake, directly across the lake from Louie, a Frenchman by the name of Sam Seymour had a cabin. He was a trapper and a woodsman, though not one to go far back into the big woods. He was good at making dugouts and had one at Lewey Lake and one at Dug Mountain Ponds. Sam was built like Louie, short and stocky, and had the same reddish brown hair and blue-black eyes. Although they had often seen each other at the lake, each one had always silently gone his own way, but one day when they met at the store in Indian Lake village, and Louie hardly noticed him, Sam edged closer to Louie near the counter until their eyes met.

"Hallo," he said. "Yo' name Seymour de sam lak mine. Ma name ees Sam. Strange ting. Two Seymour."

"Dat's no ver' strange ting. Plaintee Seymour on Canadaw."

"Dat ees true, Louie, but eet ees ver' curious ting jus' de sam. Bod come off Kebec also, you an' me."

"Dere's moche more Seymour dere."

"True enough, ma fren'. A fella he tol' me you come off Dog Reever. Me also, sam lak you."

"Dog Reever? You?"

"Sam ting." Sam eased himself against the counter. "Louie, you no tink eet ees true. You tink eet ees funny mebbe, but ah tink you ma broder."

Louie was not surprised at anything. "Wall, Dog Reever, dat's ver' long tam ago. Ba gosh, ah got moche broder an' seester dere, but ah don' 'member no broder name Sam."

Each said that their family had broken up in Canada and told the same story of a hard stepmother.

When they left the store they took the road to Lewey Lake together. From then on they saw more of each other and, before long, Sam induced Louie to come and live with him. Sam was sure Louie was his own brother and at times Louie almost believed it. But Sam's habits and manners were in many ways the opposite of Louie's. Sam did not drink and was glad to meet people and always tried to be as nice as he could to everyone. He was neat and clean. Louie could not live without his sprees and paid little attention to anyone. They lived together about a month, then Louie moved back to his own cabin, telling Sam that he would have to be getting his traps ready for setting out the lines, for the season was getting along.

Louie could not read nor write. Neither could some of the Frenchmen who even ran small stores. There is a story about one who was known simply as "Old Joe."

A man who had a small lumber job was in Joe's store checking up about a bill.

"Barrel flour," said Joe.

"Right," said the jobber.

Old Joe studied the book. "Yo' buy five bale hay."

"Five bale of hay."

"Wan baga beans."

"Bean. Right. All right, Joe."

"Wan cheese," said Old Joe.

"Cheese? What cheese? No cheese, Joe."

Old Joe shouted as he put his finger on the picture in the book. "Yo' buy wan cheese."

"You're crazy, Joe. I don't buy cheese."

"By gar, meester, dat's right. Dat cheese, she was grindstone. Ba cripe, ah forget for put hole in heem."

When it got to be too civilized for him at Lewey Lake, Louie moved on, this time to Jessup River, where he built another little cabin and stayed there for one winter. In the spring he shifted again to an old clearing on the Indian Lake-Newton Corners road. From his camp Louie went out in search of Cedar Lakes, of which he had heard during his stay at Lewey Lake, but the directions were poor and he went to Cedar River Flow and wound up at

13

Indian Lake village. Trying again, he found the lakes and blazed a trail of his own and built a little cabin and stayed at the Cedars for weeks.

He was always ready to build another camp. As trapping took him to Pillsbury Lake, he set up two sturdy barn lean-tos facing each other, with a space for a fire in between. He now lived mostly at Pillsbury and the Cedars and went out to the town of Newton Corners more than he did to Indian Lake. Then on one of these trips to the settlements he saw circus bills posted in the barrooms, on the sides of all roadside barns and inside and outside of hotel horsesheds, and he could not escape the excitement of a circus coming to town. Dates he didn't know and the day of the week never bothered him, but by the way the lumberjacks talked he knew that this was the day.

Louie left his pack and gun with Dave Sturges and went along with the others to the foothills town. He saw the main show, the minstrels, the three-headed calf and the two-headed woman. He sniffed the smell of the circus and forgot the pungent odor of spruce. After the show, in a dust that rose like mist, came the rattle of chains, the thud of hoofs, the shouting of drivers and tent men, the rumble of wagons and creaking of wheels—the great confusion of so many familiar sounds.

And he promptly forgot all about his traplines and his little cabins. He forgot all about Sam, Griffin, Dave Sturges and John Maginn, forgot all about the freedom of the wilderness country;

the call of the wild grew faint and far away. Back up in the mountains, on the shore of Cedar Lake, his little cabin looked out over the water from the shadow of the spruce, but it was indeed far from Louie's thoughts as he mixed with the tent men, asked for a job and got it. The lumberjacks went back to the woods without him.

When Louie presently headed for the woods again, for the season was well on and soon the circus put up for the winter down in New England, it was not this time the Adirondacks, but Maine, and he landed in the vicinity of Moosehead.

That winter he stayed there, but the New York woods were always in his heart. Sooner or later he was sure to come back to them.

He came back sooner than he expected. He killed a moose out of season, in the spring, and had to move quickly as the law was after him. In fact it was so close that Louie struck out cross-country, and when he came to a river full of saw-logs in a driving flood, he rode the logs, and, as he said, he left no tracks in getting out of the state of Maine.

"Ah was glad for see all dem saw-log dere," Louie told his old acquaintances at Newton Corners about it when he returned. "Ba gosh, dat was locky ting for ol' Louie. Ah jomp on wan log an' ride heem down, an' ah'll tole you, ma fren, dat man he geev oup for tink he see dem track som more."

He didn't go back to the Cedars, but settled nearer to Newton Corners, throwing together a little camp where the road north of the town crosses Hatchery Brook. It was an easy walk to the Corners, where he worked at odd jobs. A short time later he moved in and boarded with Dave Sturges while he cleared several acres of land for Dave in the village, digging out the stumps and burning the limbs.

Many of the people in the settlements worked for the nearby tanneries, and Louie saw them going to their work either in the tannery or to the woods to get out tan-bark. The bark peelers had to peel enough bark in the few weeks that the sap was running to run the tannery for a year. After the bark was removed the white

15

logs, "like the blanching bones of some army of fallen giants," were left in the woods to decay, three to six hemlocks, enough to make a thousand feet of lumber, wasted to obtain one cord of bark. The tanneries used western or South American hides that were teamed in from the nearest railroad and the leather was hauled out. The tanneries were in the woods to be near the hemlocks.

While at Newton Corners Louie fell in love, or thought he did. Some say "he married her for her horse." There was no marriage. They simply lived together at her place on a small farm down the East Road, but it did not work out so well. One season was enough. Louie belonged back in the woods, not on a farm. When it came to separation and settling up, Louie claimed a share in the few tools and the chickens that were on the place. What he took as his was of no use at all to him except to trade in at the store the very next day. He traded for provisions, traps and woods gear to take in to Pillsbury and the Cedars. Now, at last, he was going back to the Cedars. Burr Sturges was in Slacks' store at the time. So was the young boy Jim, who liked to be with these men.

"Trapping out from the Cedars, Louie?" Burr asked.

"Mebbe. Mebbe yes, mebbe no."

Burr watched him getting his outfit. "How would you like to trap with me this winter?"

Even for Louie, that was something to think about! Burr was the best trapper that went out from Newton Corners. The furs he brought in proved it. Why not trap one season with Burr?

"The West Canada Country, Louie," Burr was saying. "There's more fur there than there is around the Cedars."

"Ah don' t'ink. Mebbe."

Burr watched Louie pack his stuff. He had been in the woods with Louie and had great respect for the Frenchman's woodcraft. Country Louie had once seen, he never forgot. He didn't blaze much. Now and then he would break over some branches. Burr had followed some of Louie's lines where the blazes were low, not over two feet from the ground, a line that few could follow. They often resembled an anchor tilted one way or the other, point-

16

ing the direction, and there wouldn't be many; just in the particular places, such as where he would leave a ridge or cross a swamp or stream.

"W'en you go?" Louie asked presently, without looking up.

"Whenever you're ready," Burr told him.

"Ah go wid you."

Young boy Jim was all attentive to what went on between the two trappers. He wasn't wondering just how to say it, it just came right out: "I know how to trap. Can I go?"

Burr said, "No, Jim. You're too—you know you've got to go to school."

"When Gramp was no bigger'n me, he went way in to Indian Clearin' to drive Lyman Holmes' cattle in for him."

"That's right, boy, he did. Well, I guess maybe next year I'll stay home. You'll be big enough then, and maybe you can go with Louie, that is, if—

"Sure, next wintaire, Jeem. You trap wid me." Louie put his hand on the boy's shoulder. "You an' me, Jeem, next wintaire."

And Jim didn't forget.

So that fall of 1878 Louie trapped with Burr Sturges far back in a section that was known to only a few trappers, the West Canada Country.

Burr had a well-made enclosed camp on Lake Low, or Whitney Lake, which they used. When on North Lake or "Big West" of the West Canadas, they stayed in a little slab shanty against the big rock at the back of the clearing, the camp that Chet Sturges, Burr's brother, and Marinus Lawrence had built. When at Pillsbury they stayed at Louie's double bark lean-tos.

This was Louie's first full season around the West Canadas and he did learn the country. The following fall of 1879 Burr did not trap, but Jim, Burr's son, now a boy of sixteen and a born woodsman, took his father's place and they trapped together during that winter of 1879 and '80. Their headquarters was at the same place on Whitney and their trap lines were set far to the north, to within a mile of the Moose River and Indian Clearing.

17

It was a man's job indeed to follow those winter lines. With snowshoe and pack they left the headquarters camp, going in opposite directions, to meet again on the northern end of the lines. Each did his circle, stopping nights at small trap-line cabins, where, after getting something to eat, he skinned out the glossy mink and marten and worked late into the night fleshing the pelts. The large pelts of the otter and fisher were skinned out on the lines where caught.

From Whitney the line went first to Sampson and Sampson Bog, down the outlet to West Creek and Mica, on to Poor, north to the west of Northrup and down the Indian to Stink Lake. From Stink, it went east past Beaver and Squaw, to Falls Pond, north and up the Otter Valley, south across the swamps on upper Otter Creek, then on to the Cedars and back to Whitney. There were cross lines connecting Wolf, Twin, Brook Trout, Big West, Mud and Whitney.

At the far northwest end, Louie and young Jim met at a little cabin nearly hidden in the snow, not far from Stink Lake, where the first to arrive waited until the other came in. After one night together, with little talk between them, they went their way, traveling alone, back tracking each other and meeting again at the main camp on Whitney. They took over a week to make the round trip, and carried no rifle, no firearms of any kind, just a large hunting knife.

That winter they caught two hundred and seventy-five pine marten and sold them for around a dollar a skin. The little nocturnal animals liked the dark evergreen forests around the West Canadas and were not hard to trap, with rabbit or venison for bait. They also caught quite a few mink, some fisher cats and otter. The fisher cat was a pest to the trappers, being cunning in springing the traps. Deadfalls set for them often were left in ruins. They were a muscular animal, a tree traveler, jumping from tree to tree like a squirrel, clearing a distance of forty feet and never failing a secure grip.

Young Jim, approaching Falls Pond, came upon the tracks of two wolves. The much trampled snow showed where they had

18

killed and eaten a deer and dragged something out onto the ice. A dark spot proved to be the deer's hide, and Jim cautiously followed the wolves' tracks from the hide to the rise of ground of a nearby island. There he found their beds in the snow, where they could lie and watch the hide on the ice. Fresh tracks showed they had seen him coming and had sneaked away.

Jim went on to the trap-line cabin and that night he heard the wolves howling off toward Kitty Cobble. Louie, who was on one of the cross lines, came in the next day from Twin Lakes.

"Saw wolf sign on that island in Falls Pond," Jim told him. "Heard 'em howling."

"Ol' Louie see plaintee sign on dees leetle pon' two, t'ree mile. W't you call heem, Jeem, dat lettle pon'?"

"I dunno Louie, what do yo' call it?"

"Ah see plaintee sign dere. Ah tink she ees Wolf pon'."

"Wolf Pond she is, Louie. That she be."

On the northern end of these trap lines was the Indian Clearing, called by many the wildest section around. Sometimes Jim or Louie put up for the night in a small cabin Isaac Kenwell of Indian Lake had built. When they did, they always saw signs of wolves nearby and heard them howling. Once as Jim was approaching the cabin he saw smoke rising from the chimney. In answer to his "halloo", Kenwell came to the door. Jim stayed with him and in the evening Kenwell told of a trip when his wife came in with him for a "just once" over the trap lines with her husband before heavy snow set in. They had left William Wakely's Headquarters at Cedar River Flow and from there went to Little Moose and Silver Run, following down the Moose River. In the small log camp Isaac had slept on the front side to watch the fire and his wife had taken the bunk against the logs and chinking. She was tired but she did not sleep, for all night long the wolves were prowling around the cabin.

"Go to sleep," Kenwell told her, "they can't harm you."

She knew all was safe inside those walls of logs, but she lay there wide awake, listening until near dawn when the wolves

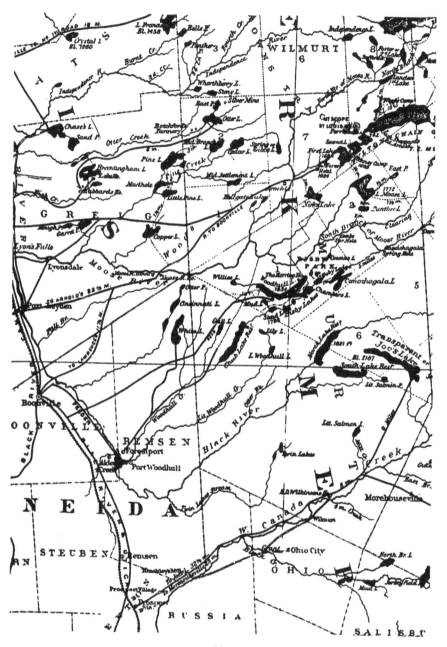

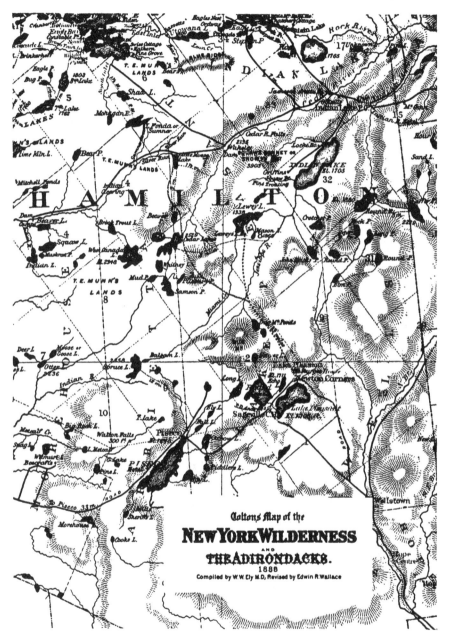

Colton's Map of the
NEW YORK WILDERNESS
AND
THE ADIRONDACKS.
1888
Compiled by W.W. Ely M.D, Revised by Edwin R. Wallace

21

went away. She then slept while her husband puttered about the cabin waiting for her to get her much needed rest.

And so Kenwell talked to Jim of other trips and of wolves and of timber. Kenwell topped them all as a timber cruiser in the north country, and Jim listened attentively.

"One time when I was up in Canada," he related. "I was estimating timber and I had a couple of Indian guides with me. We hit cross country, traveling hard so as to get through it. Grub was low, in fact almost gone. The two guides refused to go on. I argued with them telling them that I had told the company that I would get the figures, and that I could not go back without them. The guides agreed to make the cross country side trip and stay two more days on one condition. 'What's that?' I asked them, ready to grant anything reasonable, and what do you think they said, Jim?"

"More money."

"No. They said 'Food is short. We will go on if you give us time to pray.' The trip was made, Jim, and the timber estimate was brought out."

"Good."

"Do you know how to estimate timber, Jim? Well, remember that one man can't get outside of the middle of an acre, so if you stand in the woods and look one hundred and seventeen feet and eight inches in every direction, the timber you see is the amount of—listen, did you hear that?—the amount of timber per acre. Listen, Jim!"

All was quiet. Kenwell raised his finger and turned a keen ear toward the only window in the cabin. "Hear 'em? Wolves."

Jim heard them now, faint and far away.

Kenwell got up and opened the door and Jim stood beside him.

"On the plains. Well, Jim, if you're going to follow that trap line tomorrow you'd better be turning in. If you don't show up on Whitney on time Louie'll think the wolves got you."

22

Ba Da Holy Feesh

Chapter Three

In the spring, Louie and Jim brought their furs out to the Corners. After Louie had succeeded in drowning his six-month thirst, he traded for supplies and headed back in again, this time alone, packing his heavy load over the trails. This was the spring of 1880. He stopped overnight at Pillsbury and the next day rowed across the lake and followed the trail to Whitney where there was another boat ride. From the opposite shore of Whitney he went by trail to Mud Stream where he had a boat which he used to take him down the stream and across Mud Lake, then by trail to Big West and to the clearing and the little old slab shanty by the rock.

Early mornings, he took his water-pail and stepped out into the cool crisp air. The lake lay still under the low drifting mists. On the edges of the clearing he would often see deer feeding or standing stiff and alert before bounding away into the woods. Going over the path to the spring he would see and hear the woods life all about him. Let others be farmers, sailors, canalers, loggers, or circus men. Louie had been all of them. He had seen many places but no better country had he seen than this West Canada.

During that first summer he worked on the shack, evening up the floor, patching the roof, plugging the holes, battening the cracks, tightening it up against the cold that was sure to come. He cut and piled his firewood close to the door. He cleaned out his spring. The packed earth showed that there had been quite a procession to quench their thirst there before Louie took over. He poked about the clearing, looking for bits of anything that was man-made, a piece of wire, an old cooking pot. It takes years, many years, to make an honest "clearin'" but a man who hasn't much, leaves little behind and what little he does leave, nature is quick to cover up.

On his next trip to the Corners Louie brought back some real window lights to take the place of the oiled paper, cloth and skins, and he packed in a few chickens and had a coop and small yard to one side of the shanty.

He lent a hand to his one tenacious young apple tree by building a high tight sapling fence around it to protect it from the deer and hedgehogs. And he brought in some rhubarb roots, for where was there a French Canadian who did not like rhubarb?

He had a garden that produced wonderful vegetables. Watching over it, he had his own little army of "potato bug hunters," as he called them. They were snakes. Some of them he called by name. When he rapped on a board, they came out and cleaned up all the fish entrails that he tossed to them. They kept his meat block clean. He found them in his wanderings and even made special trips to the sunny grassy plains on the Moose River for the largest, and brought them back in his pack, in his pockets or inside of his shirt. Around the camp he placed overturned tin pans on the rocks in the sun for them to get under. He protected their ground dens by covering these with brush or slabs. Louie liked snakes and gave them due credit for the mammoth potatoes that he raised.

24

The snakes did not deserve all of the credit. Trout or the big suckers from Mud Lake inlets in the spring made excellent fertilizer. One can believe or not that he "planted half a ten pound lake trout in each potato hill in his garden." It is just as true that over on Indian Lake they were feeding trout to their hogs. The natives of Lewey and Indian Lakes tell how they went with horse and wagon to the stream between the two lakes when northern pike were running to spawn. With pitch-forks they filled their wagonboxes and took the loads home to feed to the hogs. In Newton Corners, not long before this, they were taking wheel barrows down to Lake Pleasant in which to bring back their catches of lake trout. During the first years that Louie was in at the West Canadas, he was not so very particular whether he used trout or suckers, but like the Indian Lake pike, the Mud Lake suckers were easier to get. Louie dug a pit which furnished much of his fertilizer. Into this pit, along with a thin covering of dirt, went entrails of deer if killed not too far from camp, woodchucks, rabbits, even small birds and squirrels, and garbage to rot. As the hole was big enough, perhaps a whole deer would now and then be dropped into it. It was rich for Louie's pie plant grew four feet tall and as big around as your wrist. He cut it in small pieces and festooned it on string to dry for winter use. Anyhow, between the snakes and the fertilizer, whether it was trout or suckers or what, Louie's garden did well. And so did Louie.

He ate fish, partridges, ducks and venison, bear meat and what he raised in his garden. Flour and meal from the settlements helped out. The seasons rolled around. Long cold winters were passed on the trap lines, when the whiskey-jacks, crossbills and chickadees were welcome visitors. In the spring he made his maple syrup with the sociable little chickadees for company and later planted his potatoes to the song of the white-throats, "la siffleur," the whistler, a little bird he had known years before in Canada. Summers he wandered exploring, fishing and building new cabins in new country. Then colder nights and shorter days, and quickly it was winter again.

A small pack of wolves hung around Twin Lakes all one winter.

Louie saw them there and spotted where they had killed deer. Some nights alone in his warm shack, when the trees surrounding the clearing were cracking like guns in the cold stillness, he heard the wolves and stepped to the door to listen to their lonesome howls and take a look at the stars, so bright and near, or the brilliant streamers of the northern lights.

Once, returning from Whitney, he was crossing the ice on the east side of Mud, and, beyond the snowy lake, saw what at first he thought were seven deer. There was one big one. "Ah keel dat beeg buck," he said to himself, and started stalking around the shore. When part way around he realized that they were wolves and cautiously tried to move closer for a better shot, but the wolves had seen him and were gone before he could get within better range. They had killed a deer and eaten it all up, bones and all, except the gambrel joints.

Louie learned the West Canada country not only by traveling it but also by listening whenever Burr Sturges or Marinus Lawrence had anything to say. Marinus Lawrence drew a map for Louie. It was drawn on brown paper pasted on to a piece of oil-cloth, and showed the main mountains and streams. With this map as a guide, Louie made maps of his own, which probably no one could interpret but himself. They were drawn on paper birch in four sections, each about eighteen inches square, and took in a larger territory, covering a country from Mud Lake to the forks of the Moose and from the Cedars to the Indian River. They showed his trails and camps, trap-lines and sets, and where

26

he had seen plenty of deer and bear or signs of marten, otter and fisher. Distances were marked on the maps by the time it took to travel between points. He kept them in a large tin can with a tight cover, and few persons ever saw them. One who did said that the lakes were all drawn round and of equal size.

Every fall Louie set his heavy bear traps and caught from two to five bear. The hides brought eight or ten dollars each. The meat was put down in brine, the same as pork. He liked bear meat. Fried potatoes and bear meat and strong tea satisfied him as well for breakfast as for supper. He ate, sitting on his bunk and picking the food with his fingers from the spider.

Louie discovered the lake trout by a sort of accident. He was fishing and had laid his rod down in the boat for a moment, when all of a sudden the line ran out to a great depth. He grabbed it and knew at once this was something bigger than any brook trout. He pulled in against the heavy strain too anxiously; the line broke and the fish was lost. But he sent outside for a spool of copper wire and with this line caught lakers that ran from twelve to twenty pounds. Many hooked later would run eight, with the heads off, to a full pack basket load. Louie, incidentally, soon preferred the laker to any brook trout for good eating.

Louie was never lazy. He made sleds from tough split saplings, and with a harness that he got into, pulled loads in through the snow from the outside, often having a load of two hundred pounds when leaving Newton Corners.

He used a sled to pull venison in to camp, but sometimes he used a deer-hide laced to each arm of a curved bow. When pulled by the curved part, the hide, hair side out, formed a bag that half dragged in the snow between the poles. It pulled easily as the two ends of the bough extended behind as runners and partly supported the load. In this way much of his venison was hauled from Wolf Creek Stillwater on the Indian, a favorite hunting ground.

His trapping camps were all well made. They were mostly the lean-to style, only about two feet high in back, and with the higher and open front built up to within a foot or so of a big rock against which he had his fire. Squared up snug and tight, many had split plank floors and plank bunks raised a little above them. Some had bark roofs, some scoops, but most of them were roofed with heavy shakes.

Besides these Louie had little camps scattered about the woods all the way from his double bark lean-tos on Pillsbury Lake to his trapping cabin on Stink Lake. For one camp in the Otter Valley he made use of a large hollow birch log. It was sealed up on the end with a door cut in the side. It was a good foul weather camp at any time of year, for in winter when the log was buried in snow except for the cleared entrance, he could close the door and light a lantern to keep him warm.*

He had a solid door over a hole in the rocks on Wolf Creek, and a camp against a big rock at Twin Ponds. At a rocky ledge a few miles east of the West Canadas, great slabs of rocks had fallen and formed a room, which though open on one side had a ceiling and three straight even walls on the others. Someone besides Louie had once used it as a camp, but he did his part by building a bunk against one of the walls. A cold spring of water flowed nearby, and it became known in time to many as "Shanty Rock."

Still another haven of his was in the cave on Cobble Hill with its litter of the ashes of old camp fires that looked as though they had been cooked over and sat around but a short time before but they were the remains of fires built by trappers who had been dead for over fifty years. What stories the shades of those old trappers could have told!

> *fightin' four hungry wolves with nothin' but my hunting knife.*
> *I'm durned if th' snow wa'n't tramped down with painter tracks all over t' clearin.*
> *Crawled out an' give that coon a kick alongside th' jaw an' knocked 'im clean off th' limb. I pounced on 'im an'*

---

* Lumbermen in the 1940's found what was left of this camp.

28

*went kersouse in th' crick but I got that coon under an'
drowned 'im.*
*we hadn't no mor'n rammed a load inter our guns when
we heerd a screech off in th' woods.*
*the crust was so slippery first thing I knowed both me
an' th' bear wus awhizzin' down th' mountain like a streak
o' chain lightnin'.*
The old cus carried off a dozen traps an' got rid o' them.

By the great horned spoon, what tales those blackened coals
could have told Louie, had they talked!

In every one of his camps he had a store of food, and all
about the woods, like a blue jay, he kept tucked away little bundles
of dry kindling and pitch-knots.

Although one of these camps was usually not so far away
that he could reach it before dark, Louie in his travels could
easily throw up a quick shelter for the night. One evening as
he made camp in the woods and prepared to kindle a fire, a blood-
curdling scream came but a few yards away.

He had encountered a panther. These "varmints," as early
settlers called them, were still plentiful in the woods. It has been
estimated that one hundred were slain in the Adirondacks between 1860 and 1882. In 1871 a law was passed to pay twenty
dollars bounty on panthers and between that year and '82 forty-
six were paid. Large as they were and in spite of the fate of the
boy driver on the canal who was said to have been carried off by
one, the big cats shunned a human being. Louie heard his visitor
leaving abruptly, passing noisily among the branches from tree to
tree. A panther would, however, jump from a considerable
height in a tree on to the back of a deer. A month or so later
Louie killed a deer the back of which showed the scars of wounds
extending from shoulder to tail. As the deer dashed madly
among the trees, a stout limb had evidently scraped the panther
clean off its back.

So Louie, finally following his bent, had established himself
as part of a chosen wilderness. He merged himself with it but

at least twice a year went out to the Corners and for two or three weeks both amused the tiny town and taxed its patience, whooping it up until his money was gone. It was amazing how quickly nearly a thousand dollars, gained from the sale of furs that represented a winter's steady trapping, could disappear at the tavern that was lucky enough to get his business.

On one of his return trips he had salt pork in his pack. He was quite unsteady, when, just before climbing Blue Ridge, he settled down on some matted grass in the sun. It was a good spot to rest and sleep it off. The spring air was quiet and warm and Louie lay for a long time. When he reached around to adjust the shoulder straps he thought he had lost his pack. The hedgehogs had eaten up all of his salt pork and even a good part of the basket! They had eaten it right off his back.

By Buckboard and Trail

Chapter Four

After 1880 outsiders began coming into the West Canada country. The wonderful fishing was becoming known to sportsmen. In Brook Trout Lake the speckles were "packed like sardines." In Big West were the huge "lakers."

At first not so many sportsmen ventured into the section as the long stage and buckboard trips were slow and tiresome over the worst sort of roads. But as railroads were built, more arrived at the foothill towns of North Creek, Northville and Prospect, from which "jumping off places" they continued on in by stage. They always came out with stories of great catches. For instance:

"During our second visit we reached the head of the stillwater in time to select a camping site and construct a bark lean-to to make ourselves comfortable for the night," one piece of correspondence ran. "The rain continued next day. We remained in camp while the guides built and floated a raft. It was still raining in the afternoon but we were determined to fish and as we could not escape a wetting we concluded to wade. The stillwater boiled with ravenous trout. The four of us caught them so rapidly that we did not move one hundred yards from camp before we had more trout than we could use. We found that we had taken two hundred and fifty trout in less than two hours." This report goes on to say that next morning the guide left camp and packed the fish out to Morehouseville to save them.

Another reports: "Here the stream had cut a long and deep channel under the heavy alders overhanging the opposite bank. This was the lurking place of the large trout. When the sun did not throw your shadow upon the water you could cast the fly from the meadow with the certainty of landing nothing less than a half-pounder."

And such as this, something to write home about: "The tall grass bent over the brook and made it appear less than a rod wide. Before fishing we were in the habit of dropping our hooks into the water to moisten the catgut. We followed this plan and each fisherman caught a trout on a bare hook. We tried again with the same result. Then we decided to dangle the bare hook three or four inches over the water in order to avoid catching the small trout. In less than an hour our baskets were filled with beautiful trout. The fact that this vlei was at least ten miles from the nearest habitation accounted for the superabundance of trout."

And this: ". . . a mountain lake with crystal waters reflecting the deep blue of the heavens. Its northern edge runs along the foot of a steep mountain. The deep water is found near this shore and from the trunk of a huge pine tree that had been felled into the lake one seldom failed to catch a fine mess of trout. On the morning of breaking camp we fished an hour and took out with us nine trout weighing eleven pounds."

With such sport afforded, some of the visiting parties of fishermen soon became regulars. Even though they came for but a few days, several times a year, rough camps were thrown

FRENCH LOUIE

EARLY ADIRONDACK HOME

THE PILLSBURY LAKE CAMP
LOUIE AT HIS FIRST CAMP

FRONT AND BACK OF LOUIE'S CAMP
AT WEST CANADA LAKE

THE WILSON CAMP ON WEST CANADA LAKE

CAMP BUILT FOR DR. RALPH,
THE ORNITHOLOGIST

Photo by E. A. Spears

THE FERRIS CAMP ON THE WEST CANADA CREEK,
JUST ABOVE BUCK POND STILLWATER

THE NINHAM CAMP AT THE HEAD OF
THE SECOND STILLWATER

AT THE FOOT OF THE FIRST STILLWATER, 1888

THE CAMP AT THE FOOT OF THE
SWANSON OR FIRST STILLWATER

INDIAN LAKE VILLAGE

ORDWAY'S NORTH CREEK STAGE
in front of the Commercial Hotel
Indian Lake

Courtesy of Gretchen M. Fish

THE NORTHVILLE STATION

THE NORTHVILLE STAGE AT BROOKS'
HOTEL IN SPECULATOR

On the F. J. & G.
They came to Northville

ADIRONDACK STAGES

THE HOSLEY HOUSE
at Wells, where the stages stopped
for dinner and to change horses

Courtesy of Vurner Pilchard

HUNTING PARTY READY TO LEAVE NORTHVILLE.
EVERY MAN HAD HIS DOG

SOMETIMES IT WAS UNHITCH, UNLOAD AND
REPAIR A BROKEN SLED IN THE WOODS

PULLING OUT OF SLED HARBOR

TEAM AND SLED AT LOUIE'S

SLED HARBOR
Sometimes there were twenty or thirty
old and new sleds lying around

THE NORTHVILLE-PISECO STAGE
Watering the horses at the Forks below Wells

THE MOHAWK RIVER BRIDGE
BETWEEN UTICA AND DEERFIELD
where the N. Y. Central R. R.
tracks are now

together and presently took on a permanent appearance. The "Wilson Camp," built and owned by two brothers from the city of Oneida, was a semi-open log and bark camp near the head of Louie's own Big West. On a very small stillwater of the West Creek, not far below where the outlet of Mica Lake comes in, there was a small enclosed hut called "Ferris Camp." It was about twelve feet square, built of upright logs covered with bark, had a bark roof and an inside fireplace. It was right on Louie's old trap line, and a good spring hole in front of it was known as the "Ferris Spring Hole," from which many a beautiful trout was taken. Another camp of the visiting sportsmen was the "Ninham Camp," an open lean-to with a smaller lean-to adjoining, located at the head of the second West Creek stillwater on the south side in the big bend.

Now Louie was a man of the woods. He knew his way around when the icy winds swept across the Indian Clearing, the lakes and the frozen stillwaters; when the woods were drenched in fog or when the swollen streams flooded the low places and blocked the way. And he was strong, active, tireless on the trail; an expert with an axe, quick and sure with a rifle. He was not afraid of man or beast nor of discomfort nor hardship. He was contented and got much out of life. Even fighting his way back to camp in bleak wind and rain or biting cold gave him a strange sense of pleasure. And he had good habits in the woods. He did not drink whiskey in camp, did not even smoke or swear. He cared little for the outside world, except of course his periodic sprees. Politics meant nothing to him, he never discussed creeds, but he was honest and believed in the gospel of hard work. Although he was sensitive to ill treatment and never forgot an injury, he was highly appreciative of kindness, loved his friends warmly and was ever loyal to them. There was always a twinkle in his eyes.

It is no wonder that the outsiders began making arrangements for his skill at guiding and for the use of his camps. For this they paid generously. Since they would not hurt his trapping, he soon lost any resentment he may have had of them.

33

Even when some of these invaders of his solitudes put up for the night in his lean-tos at Pillsbury Lake and burned them down from the sparks thrown by a fire of dead soft wood, not the safe steady blaze of the singing steaming green birch, he did not wait long before building another camp. He had to have a place for the visitors and he set to work to get out logs for a bigger better place than he ever had anywhere. The red spruce grew tall and plentiful around Pillsbury, and he built a large, roomy camp, solidly made and roofed with wide shakes. The fact that he owned no land never bothered him. In back of the camp a ramp led to a door on the second floor large enough for a horse to walk through. The floor rested on ten and twelve inch logs. The ramp was about eight feet wide made of split logs round side up.

As there was indeed so much about "French Louie," as he came to be called at this time, that made the outsiders want to be with him, it was to be expected that this likable and interesting backwoods character would be getting into print. The following appeared in a New York City newspaper:

"Out at the settlement of Newton Corners, twenty-five miles distant from West Canada by waterways and trail, Louie Seymour was indulging in his accustomed six weeks semi-annual relaxation. He had come out of the woods with his winter's catch of fur and at once proceeded, as was his wont, to convert prime pelts of mink and marten, fisher and otter, into the red spirits which befuddle the brain, yet gladden the heart.

"Like Jack ashore, he was acclaimed in his accustomed haunts. Louie was at such times ever a liberal host and his cronies in consequence suffered little from thirst.

"His presence was less welcome, however, to the timid women of the little hamlet and to the skittish horses which had occasion to pass his favorite resort. In a humped posture in his chair on the porch of the tavern his smoky eyes would open, and, springing from his seat, he would stretch his squat figure like a rooster at dawn, his voice breaking forth meanwhile in unearthly imitation of the calls of the forest neighbor. His repertoire ranged from the scream and hoot of the big owls to the howl of the wolf, disquieting offerings to the peace-loving community.

"All joys have a termination. It was so with Louie's sprees. As was usual toward the end of his drinking bouts, he was now roused to a degree of sobriety by his maudlin outpourings of compassion for the bears suffering torture in the traps set on Indian River with possible thought of good fur going to waste.

"On the morrow he would go in to the West Canada and put out of misery such of the bears as might be living. Big John Sturges who could carry the Canadian through to his destination in his pack basket and who proposed going into the woods to paint his boats, volunteered to convey the rum-shaken trapper.

"At sunrise next morning as Uncle David Sturges, mighty old time moose hunter, trapper and guide, was putting an hour of practice at croquet on the ground alongside his homelike hotel in the effort to retain the hotly contested championships, Louie passed up the road, pack on back and accompanied by his promised escort, John Sturges, and as the pair mounted Nat Page's hill and disappeared over the brow, Dave fervently murmured, 'Thank God he is gone! Now Newton Corners can sleep.'

"Mile after mile the two woodsmen left the village behind, as well as the drinking debts of Louie to payment of which the summer and fall guiding would be devoted.

"By the fish hatchery—where a hatchery was not then a crying necessity—their route carried them, with a pause later at Whiskey Brook, where Louie permitted none of nature's beverage to reduce the potency of the bottled nectar which snuggled by the side of the restoring Jamaica Ginger in the pack basket.

"Crossing the Jessup River on the pole bridge, passing the Lewey Lake turn, through Sled Harbor into the 'Hell Hole' and up the back-breaking Blue Ridge, they continued, and then down the mountain to Pillsbury Lake, and through the length of this lake by rowboat, with deer feeding on every side.

35

At the foot of Pillsbury Lake the boat was pulled out and resuming their packs the two followed the trail to West Canada Lakes. Over a rise in the land and across a quaking bog the path led, and early in the afternoon they broke out of the woods and stood on the shore of beautiful, wild little Whitney Lake, eight or nine miles east of West Canada with numerous timbered islands and borders of virgin spruce.

"Launching a boat they entered it and started upon the row across the lake, John's huge bulk in the stern facing forward and shoving on the oars, while Louie sat perched in the uplifted bow like a lookout in a crow's nest.

"Halfway across the lake Louie called to the oarsman, 'Hey John, push up to dat gull rock. Ba cripe! I'm thirsty. Goin' to make an egg nog.'

"John propelled the boat to the indicated spot, and as the female gull on the nest and the mate on the water took wing, and, flying above the intruders, voiced their feelings over the contemplated robbery, Louie thrust in his hand and filched an egg from the nest. He unfastened the tin cup attached to his belt and laid the cup on his lap and reaching into his pack basket produced the depleted whiskey bottle. Pouring a generous portion of the liquor he broke the shell of the egg on the rim of the cup and dropping in the contents stirred the mixture with a dirty digit.

"He was on the point of raising the drink to his expectant lips when the amusement of John at the gastronomic venture of his partner was turned into horror by the stage of incubation of the egg which he had only just noted.

" 'Hold on, Louie!' cried John, 'there's a bird in it.'

"Louie Seymour directed his bleared eyes for a moment upon the concoction, then leering to his companion, replied, " 'Dat's alright, John. Ba cripe! I'm hungry too,' whereupon he gulped down the succulent egg nog."

36

Old Kate Dog

Chapter Five

It was in the hunting and trapping, rather than the fishing that Louie's chief activity and source of income lay. Each spring he would tote out to the settlements great loads of deer hides and the pelts of fur bearing animals, the sale of which defrayed the cost of his annual sprees and his meagre necessities.

In those early days conservation was very young, or something merely talked about, and no restrictions limited the destruction of the deer, no quota per hunter, no ban on running them down with dogs.

Before hard winter set in, the deer migrated from the West Canada section where there was much green timber, to the cobble-knolls and flats north of Otter Valley and to the level Indian Clearing country where they gathered in big herds. As Dave Sturges told, they made runways like packed horse-trails between the green timbered country and the better feed north. On moonlight nights in the fall men placed themselves at picked spots and shot hundreds of deer just for the hides. It was far back in and the meat was left to rot in the woods, and this too when hides were bringing as low as fifty cents each.

When the snow lay four to six feet deep on the level the deer were to be found in yards, where hundreds of them tramped the same paths to reach a little balsam or some birch twigs to keep themselves from starving. They grew poor, so many and not enough feed to go around. The weakest fell and snow drifted over them. The month of March came, like darkness before dawn, bringing heavy snows and sleet and torturing crusts. They could not travel. Food in the yards became more scarce. The larger deer, the ones that could reach the farthest, survived.

Into many of the yards killers came on snowshoes with packs or pulling handsleighs. There were faint bleats, dripping sheath knives and red stains on white snow as these men packed their hides.

Others hunted for the market, hauling and carrying deer to the edge of the woods to sell at the nearest roads to buyers with wagons or sleighs with bark-racks in which to stack the carcasses. Many sleigh loads went over the roads through North Creek and Wells, through Grant and Gang Mills, and down through Remsen. All the main roads carried such traffic. One native at Indian Lake by the name of Hoxie hauled two loads of venison every week to the big hotels at Saratoga.

Louie did of course kill deer in the winter yards as others did, but he also skinned many that had been winter killed, so that with what the sportsmen had given him, he could accumulate many skins and come out of the woods with such loads that certain jealous guides and trappers were ready to accuse him of almost anything.

But he was also a saviour of deer. He went into the winter yards and worked days with an ax, chopping down browse for the starving deer to feed on. One summer he saved two deer from perishing in the quicksands of Twin Lakes. Seeing the deer struggling and slowly sinking, he tried to help them, but could do nothing until he hurried to a nearby trapline cabin and brought back an ax. He then felled trees and lay a matting of branches for them to get a footing on and he stayed there pulling and helping until the two exhausted deer were on firm ground where he left them too weak to travel. Louie watched them from the trees. They rose and fell down again and again and finally they stood up and slowly walked off into the spruce.

The popular way to hunt deer was with dogs. The merits of this method were being debated, and the various arguments may be summed in such a conversation as the following which may be imagined as occurring in the Pillsbury camp, after a good day's hunting, with the supper table cleared, another chunk or two put on the fire and pipes lighted:

"What do you think of a law that limits the hounding of deer to between September tenth and October eleventh?"

"Gonna spoil a lot of good sport."

"Maybe old Fenton's right. Maybe using dogs will kill off your deer. Who knows?"

"Aw, there's lots of deer."

"There may be lots of deer but how about when hounds are caught running out of season. They kill plenty."

"Dogs only hunt deer when led by a guide."

"Why, a man who was drawing logs near Morehouseville told me that while looking for a lumber-road he found eleven dead deer killed by dogs on less than two acres of ground. It was in the stiff snow and the deer were just mired and the dogs could butcher them at their leisure."

"Probably wolves."

"This fellow knows dogs' work when he sees it. Old Sam Dunning said it was nothing for a hound to go into the woods and be gone a month hunting on his own hook. I know a fellow who had a big hound he used to let run loose, and when the dog came home with bloody chops and a full belly, he would knock off work, take his hired man, and go and look for the remnant of the deer."

39

"Anyway, I'm in favor of hounding. You don't have to work yourself to death and it's not so hard on the deer either as they say it is. They say that venison is ruined by running them with dogs. They're all wrong. Anyone who is acquainted with the subject knows very well that a dog never goes at a speed of more than three or four miles an hour when running deer through the woods. Why, a deer with a broken leg can outrun a dog. A deer can escape without going one quarter of the time. It is all easy enough to talk about wanting to increase the number of deer and the cruelty of hounding and all that but they only argue that because they want the deer for you city people to kill."

"Us city people to kill! What they got to do is stop all you fellows from market hunting. Driven deer are unfit for market anyway, especially if September and October are warm. Stop the market hunting."

"Hold on now, you fellows. Did you hear about over on Fulton Chain where two guides with their hounds drove a deer into the water and one guide stayed with the deer while the other went to the hotel nearby and very kindly invited an invalid man boarding at the hotel to go out and shoot the deer. But this sick man didn't possess the so-called true water butchering instincts for he declined with disgust."

"Then the guide goes and gets a woman. I heard about that."

"Yeah. He went back to the hotel and got a woman and rowed her to where she could put a charge of buckshot in that deer."

"Then I suppose she went back to the city to show off the deer that she killed in the great North Woods."

"It's gettin' to be a real fad with 'em to shoot off a rifle. Some want to go after deer who never before had a gun in their hand."

"I heard one once call the stock a handle."

"I hope that women don't get to comin' in here to Louie's." On that they agreed and climbed up the ladder to bed.

But still talking. "You know there's two kind of deer in the woods."

"Women, I suppose, and the four legged ones," came a voice from a bunk in the corner.

"What are you talking about? There's only one kind of deer in these woods, the white tailed Virginia deer."

"There's a larger deer than the Virginia deer. He's short legged and stockily built. I've seen 'em. They are slow in running but they're strong in fighting and they are not afraid of dogs either. Instead of running away before the hounds the way your Virginia deer does they will turn and battle it out and it's a good lucky dog that don't show up missing."

"Any of 'em around here?"

"Will you guys quit talking and go to sleep?"

"Yes, they're 'round here."

"Hey, are you guys gonna hunt tomorrow? Shut up and blow out that lantern."

The room is dark. The men are half asleep when one lying near a partly opened window hears some animal prowling around outside in the garbage pile, probably a hedgehog, perhaps a bear.

"Get-out-o'them-guts," he bawls out into the night.

Soon, once again, all is quiet except for the faint crackling of the fire in the chunk stove, mice chewing among some papers downstairs and the heavy breathing of the tired hunters.

Louie did not use a dog when deer hunting alone, but only when he was with a party. He had various ones at different times but old Kate was the best. She was a small dog, mostly hound, part bird dog, weighing fifty to sixty pounds, and she was not only a deer dog but a good bear dog too, who could find one when denned up or smell one a half or three quarters mile away and come back to camp and get Louie. In woodcraft she seemed to know as much as a man.

When Louie started Kate to running a deer into Big West,

41

he would take her across in a boat and start her on the north side toward Kitty Cobble. To put her out for South Canada Lake he would take her to, the south side of North Lake, and when he wanted to start Kate running a deer into Mud Lake he would put her out on the height of land up the Pillsbury trail.

Kate brought in the deer. Louie knew the runways and knew where they would come out. Usually the watchers would not have to wait long, but sometimes they would have to sit for hours while Kate was working back in the woods. "Old Kate Dog" was working for Louie and he knew that she would bring in the meat.

The deer were wise too when the dogs were driving them. Just before they came to an opening or a place on the lake where they had been hunted before, they would often leave the runway and cross either to one side or the other and not in the runway itself.

Louie had fetched Kate in from the settlements but Bill Courtney, a guide of Piseco, had good reason to believe that Louie had just "found" her in the woods, for once when he was running deer up West Canada way, he missed his dog. He went over to Louie's to inquire and found Louie sitting in his kitchen door eating out of a spider. Bill accepted a bite of deer meat and asked if Louie had seen his dog. No, Louie told him, he hadn't seen any dog. At other times when the dog had been lost, Bill had shot off his gun, and the dog, if he was anywhere near, would answer, so now he went down to the lakeshore and shot. A dog barked, sounding as though it was on an island out in the lake. Bill took one of Louie's boats and rowed over, and there was the dog.

When he came back he was going to have it out with Louie.

"What's the idea of putting my dog out on that island?"

"Oh, dat dog," Louie said surprised. "Ba gosh, ah tink dat dog he belong to dem dam Frenchmen."

That was all the satisfaction that Bill Courtney got out of

Louie. He never knew just what "dam Frenchmen" Louie meant but thought he referred to a community near Piseco Lake.

When Louie went to town he usually left Kate in camp. Newton Corners heard that he was mistreating the dog on these occasions, and one who went in to the West Canadas found the dog on a long chain with a large kettle filled with water sunk into the ground just within reach at one end of the dog's run and at the other end was a pile of corn-bread and meat. Kate seemed satisfied.

It was on the trap line that Louie spent much of the winter, a lone figure as he followed the route along the Indian, around Wolf and Cat and down to the Moose River. There was no one within many miles. This section was remote in summer, in winter it was frozen solitude.

On his traplines Louie often caught some young animal that he would take back to camp as a pet. Once, he caught a young fisher, called a "kit fisher," that is, one born that same year in February. The fur known as "baby silk" was worth better than fifty dollars, while an old one brought around twenty. He brought it back to camp alive and for a while he thought he would be successful in taming it. As he sat and held it on his knee, the little fisher would nuzzle and paw in a kittenish way but in a month or so it lost its playful manner, became irritable and cranky, and had fits so that Louie had to kill it.

Another time at the start of the trapping season, Louie caught a large buck fisher cat in one of his traps. Camp was not so far away and he decided to take it back alive. He was partial to fishers, those cousins of the wolverine that are "fightin' devils", hard to handle. He took off his pants, tied the legs into hard knots and after fastening them on to the end of a stout stick, he poked the pants into the fisher's face, just once, and the animal's teeth set firmly into the cloth. A fisher is like a bulldog for hanging on. Louie pushed the fisher's head into a bag and quickly he tied the bag up, the same knot holding the animal's hind legs to the stick so that he could not get too active. He put the bag, stick, pants and all into his pack basket and went

43

back to camp through the woods in his underwear with the live fisher in the pack on his back. This fisher was quite an attraction for those who came to the camp that fall until he killed it for the fur.

Fisher, like panthers, killed porcupines by biting them in the belly. It was their favorite food and they swallowed many quills that must have worked through the flesh, for in skinning a fisher the layer under the hide would often be full of quills, but it was a queer thing that a quill was never found imbedded in the flesh. Fishers do not catch fish like mink and otter but live on hedgehogs, squirrels and rabbits, and, as Louie said, whatever they could steal from his traps. Hedgehog was used for bait for the traps and he would sometimes drag one through the snow where a fisher would follow the scent of it. The well-sweep or the dead-fall was the type of trap which he mostly used for fisher.

It was in the spring, just as the ice was beginning to break up, and Louie was going over his trap-line at Samson Bog. Kate was with him. They worked along the shore and at an open hole of black water they came upon a big otter caught in one of the traps. Kate dog was all excited as Louie chopped a maple sapling, trimmed a stout club and eased himself down the bank toward the otter. As he stepped over a sharp pitch of overhanging snow he grasped a small dead stub to steady himself. The stub broke off and Louie slipped and slid into the water-hole with the otter. The otter made a lunge at him and amid the splashing commotion Kate was barking and leaping about the hole. As the otter turned from Louie to Kate, Louie quickly pulled himself up the bank. He approached the hole again carefully and with two or three hard clouts with the maple club finished mister otter. A trapping cabin was near by where he dried his clothes, skinned the otter and told Kate how much he appreciated what she had done. He was always talking things over with Kate.

Louie's section was, perhaps, the best in the entire woods and the best part of his territory was along the stillwaters of the Indian, the Indian that flows north into the Moose. He caught a great amount of fur and went out with pack loads worth hundreds of dollars. He would get from twenty-five to fifty fisher from October to April. They brought from thirty to fifty dollars each. Marten sold for from a dollar and a half to two dollars and otter from ten to twenty dollars. The price of fur would, of course, vary some each year. Louie had trappers on all sides of him, but they respected his territory and kept to their own lines. There was Burt Conklin to the south of him and Nat Shepard off toward Jocks. Burt was a hard worker. He was married and had a little place in Wilmurt. After going into the woods in the fall with supplies to his headquarters camp on Shirt-tail Brook, which flows into the South Indian, he would come out just once, at Christmas time, before coming out in the spring. He got plenty of fur but he didn't turn it in on a spree like Louie. He had to share the proceeds with a team of horses and a few cows and a lot of chickens.

Raymond Spears, who calls Burt an "unadulterated wild-crafter", tells this about him.

"One spring a party came in to Burt's place in Wilmurt. For years Burt had had a big team of horses, five or six head of cattle, a hundred chickens, a dog or two. But now the barn was empty, no dogs were around, there were no chickens to speak of, just a few hens.

45

" 'What's happened, Burt?'

" 'Waal, I'll tell yo',' he laughed. 'I brought out better than seven hundred dollars worth of furs this winter. I sold 'em and turned around and paid the feed bills for them darned chickens, cows and horses! I'd worked all winter to support a lot o' live-stock! I sold the whole caboodle. Been doin' it all my life. Support a team o' horses all year to get ten dollar's worth of plowin' done come spring. And haulin' feed for them hens! No more.' "

Louie never touched anyone else's traps if they had half a right to be set where they were. If he found something in them, he might kill the animal and hang it on a bush, but to jerk a trap and steal it or the fur, is one thing that Louie never did.

Besides the two-legged hunters in that wilderness, there were the four-legged ones, whose mournful voices could be heard on cold winter nights. A pack of wolves made their home around the West Canadas and Louie often saw them. One day when he was returning on snowshoes from his long line of traps, he reached the lake just at dusk and rounding the point on a swinging dog-trot so as to get to his camp by dark, came suddenly on a large buck which had been run down by the wolves. They had torn open his throat and drunk his blood when Louie pulled out his knife ran toward them, yelling and swinging the club which, with the knife, were the only weapons that he carried. His yell-ing scared them away and, he succeeded in keeping them off until he had cut out a hindquarter. Then he made for camp and got his gun and a lantern and went back to kill the wolves. Though he was gone less than an hour, nothing was left but well picked bones.

In two years' time Louie and the parties who came in to his camp lost ten dogs while hounding deer. It was believed by most of the parties that the dogs were lost by following deer into other territory where they were taken in by guides or hunters finding them. Louie, remembering Stink Lake, thought different, and his guests knew different too after the death of Benage Paige's famous deer hound "Old Music."

46

Benage Paige, a guide from Lake Pleasant, had "Old Music" in the West Canada country. Between Big West and South Lake is South Mountain. Benage started Old Music on a fresh track. Snow was fresh and some three inches deep. The track swung right up South Mountain through the open hardwood timber which lay for nearly a mile like a park, giving full view of the dog; Benage stood in admiration watching the dog going so fast and giving voice every few jumps. As it disappeared in a cleft in the mountain, Benage started for his boat to await a chance of the deer taking a turn for the lake, but stopped at hearing Music change his bay to a howl of pain. The day was as still as some fall days when sounds can be heard miles away. Benage heard snarling and sharp barks and then saw Old Music come into view, with two wolves at his flanks. Benage instantly yelled at the top of his voice and fired his gun, which scared the wolves away. The old dog came reeling down the mountain, dyeing the snow with his blood at every jump. His strength gave out before he reached his master who was hastening to him. Benage found him bitten through the back of the neck, but the fatal wound was just back of the fore-shoulder, where a chunk of meat as large as one's hand had been torn out, laying the lungs bare. He lived but an hour.* After that, when one of Louie's dogs did not come back, they mostly agreed that it had been killed by wolves.

One means of income, though a slight one, for Louie was picking spruce gum. There was a ready market for this, as the day of prepared chewing gum had not arrived. But Louie was never what one would call a real gum picker. He picked good gum when he saw it as he was going about the woods on other business. He traded it in at the store or at one of the hotels where a picker like Tim Crowley would get it. Tim was a typical gum picker, covering territory as far north as Big Moose and Twitchell. When he wasn't away in the woods, Piseco was his home.

On logging operations Tim would pick gum from logs in

---

* From *Forest and Stream*, 1887, by M. S. Northrup, Johnstown, N. Y.

the yards, the rollways, the skidways, the booms, anywhere. The logs he picked his gum from came out of the woods from all directions, down the Moose and Black, down the West Creek and down the Jessup and Hudson. At the mills he noted logs well covered with gum and found out what section of the woods they came from.

Sometimes Tim bought gum from Louie at West Canada Lake for forty or fifty cents a pound and carried it out and sent it away, selling it to a firm down east for a dollar a pound. In the woods Tim would have a center shack from which he would carry the gum out in hundred pound loads.

To get it from the trees he used a four or five foot stick with a chisel point on the end of it. A file ground down made a good point. On the stick, just below the point, a tin can was fastened to catch the gum. The stick had a ferrule on the lower end, and into this, a pole which was easily found and fitted in the woods, could be inserted so as to reach the gum higher up. Tim usually carried a gunnysack tied with a rope over his shoulder. He and a partner picked twelve hundred pounds in a couple of months around Dug Mountain Ponds.

Louie also sold rough, uncleaned gum indirectly to Daniels of Boonville. Daniels bought gum with the bark still on it, just as it came from the trees, at eight cents a pound. He purified it by placing it on a large slanting metal plate; when heated by a fire underneath, the gum would drip off the lower edge into water where the drop-shaped pieces would suddenly cool and harden. These were packed in little cardboard boxes with sprucy Adirondack labels and sold in drug stores in all the large cities.

To Louie, the hides and furs and gum meant a good time out at the Corners. He paid up all of his old bills as soon as he came to town—his credit was always good—and in a few days there was nothing left to show for the hardest kind of work of following the trap lines during the long winter months in all kinds of weather. After he had gone back again into the woods, some one of the hotel keepers would buy a new team or build an addition.

If mail came for Louie it would be held for him until someone was going in. If Louie came to town the postmaster took it over to him where someone would have to read it and explain what it was all about. It might be from a fur dealer in Gloversville or from not too familiar sport wanting to engage Louie's services.

Louie did not always come out of the woods when those on the outside thought he was due. They looked forward to his coming; they figured on it. There was rivalry for his trade, if it could be called "trade", at times enough to start someone into the woods in search of him, to come out with him and steer him to the "right" place. Sometimes he would turn his money over to the bartender, who, pretending to mark the figures down in a book, told him when it was gone. At Cockran's Hotel Louie turned furs into credit and proceeded to buy drinks for his many friends but after several rounds he bought only for himself until Cockran swung Louie across his shoulder and carried him upstairs and dropped him onto a bed.

The bar was always busy when Louie was there. He was the center of attraction, shuffling around in his socks or bare feet and breaking out every now and then shouting. "Louie, da boy! Louie, da boy!" His swearing was no worse than "Ba cripe" and "Ba da holy feesh." When sober he did not smoke or chew, but when on one of these sprees, he chewed up the cigars that were given him, or a whole mouthful of Bull Durham. He

49

fed in the hotel kitchens alone at a side table, where he could eat with a spoon and with his fingers, just as he ate in camp. Wilderness noises came from upstairs windows, from the barroom and from the porch as Louie stuck up his head and let out an awful pantherlike screach or sent the howl of the wolf through the little town, or the hoot of an owl, the cry of a loon or hawk or wild cat.

The children in school studying their three "Rs" knew when Louie was in town. Some boy with sharp sensitive ears would be first to whisper loudly. "Louie," and the children could hardly wait for school to let out when they ran for the village store. Louie would call to them, "Ba cripey, kids, come an' get it." He liked children. They followed him into the store and gathered around him at the glass candy case as he spent his money, a

"WE ALL FISH." AT BARBER'S

dollar and a half or two dollars worth of candy, all at one time, as though nothing was too good for the kids. Horehound and lemon drops from the wooden pails were too much like medicine. It was pink wintergreen hearts, nigger babies, jackson balls and sticks with red and white spiral bands for the girls, and "lick-rish" sticks and shoe strings and white cigarettes with red glowing tips for the boys.

At other times a rangy boy with hair over his eyes and pants a mile too big for him would strut around exhibiting proudly a cheek full of jerked venison.

"Hey, Pants, where'd ja get da jerky?" some youngster would want to know. "Where's Louie? Where's Louie?" And off they would go for you could bet your bottom dollar that Louie was somewhere near with a bundle of jerky. What he didn't give to the kids he sold to the hotels for a dollar a pound.

Speaking of pants, it was interesting to see Louie buy a pair from a wandering clothes pedlar. He knew good cloth and he just pointed at them and said, "Gimme dat wan" with little thought as to size except to make sure that they were plenty large enough. He sometimes rolled the bottoms up, but more likely, he cut them off and tied a string around them, and pulled a piece of rope around his middle for a belt.

He always had something to sell when he came out; deerhides, furs, jerked venison, trout, maple sugar or spruce gum. There were those in town to whom he liked to give presents of some nice trout, maple sugar or jerky.

The people at the Corners really thought a lot of Louie, but after about two or three weeks they were weary of him and were glad when he began to think that he should be getting back again into the woods to look after his many camps. Someone usually went in with him, to see that he got in all right. Marinus Lawrence and his son Sam, then about twelve years old and on his first trip to the West Canadas, were with him on one trip, when near Hatchery Brook Louie lay down in the grass.

51

" 'Ol Louie sleep here," he said. He pointed up the brook. "Dat camp, she fall down but de roof she's good."

Marinus and young Sam propped up the roof of Louie's old camp, which was a few hundred feet up Hatchery Brook, and they slept there that night. The next night the three of them stayed at the Pillsbury camp and the third day arrived at the West Canadas.

The Corners felt that it sort of had to look out for Louie.

Barber's on Jocks Lake

Chapter Six

Louie was at the West Canada Lakes for nearly five years before those on the West Creek side of the woods knew he was there.

In the fall of 1885 he stepped out of the woods at the old Ninham camp at the head of the Second Stillwater and as he stood on a flat rock on the shore he saw a guide boat with four men in it drift quietly around the point into the big bend. He jumped back quickly out of sight into the foliage, like a wild animal sensitive about being disturbed in its solitude.

In the boat were A. D. Barber, who ran the hotel on Jocks Lake, and three of his guides; his head guide Frank Baker, Eddie Robertson, and Jim "Flannel" McMasters. They had seen Louie and Barber swore that there was a crazy man loose in the woods. They landed and McMasters found a bear trap set at the foot of the rifts and tried to follow tracks that went away from it.

When they returned to Jocks Lake, they told of seeing "a wild bewhiskered man who ran like a scairt rabbit as soon as he was seen." Then Barber's guides learned that a camp or two had been built at West Canada Lakes, so, during the fishing season, a party of them made the trip up there to try to get another glimpse of the "wild man" and to see what changes were taking place in that part of the wilderness. They traveled near the stream, past Buck Pond or Third Stillwater where they were mixed up in some thick tangled merciless going before they eventually came out at Mud Lake. They went on to the lower end of South Lake, along the sandy beach and across the shallow outlet, and in another ten minutes were at the back of the clearing on Big West. They found Louie's camp but no one was home. He had seen them coming and kept out of sight, for he was still suspicious of strangers in the woods; they might mean no good. But on later trips to the West Canadas, these parties from Barber's came to know Louie well. They were friendly and were always welcome as they paid Louie generously for the use of his camp and boats. And he gradually became accustomed to seeing more people in his section of the wilderness.

As time went on, he wanted to explore those lower West Creek stillwaters and see the Jocks Lake that he had been hearing about. He knew that black deep stillwater, bordered with spruce and overhung with alders, which lay a few miles down the West Creek, since the first year he had trapped there with Burr Sturges; and the mile of rifts below it to the head of another stillwater, where there was an open camp at the big bend and a broad view over the flat marshes to the mountains of heavy green timber to the north.

So Louie went that way carrying a light canoe and pack. He soon came to the familiar Ninham open camp in the bend, where he stopped for a few minutes before putting the canoe into the water. It was a small nine foot canoe which he had bought from Buyce and carried in from the Corners. He put his pack in the bow and as there were no seats in it, sat carefully on the bottom with his legs stretched out in front of him. It tipped easily but he was used to its crankiness.

He paddled down the mile-long stillwater. The narrow flats of heavy marsh grass between the woods were purpled with Joe Pye weed and the cardinal flower blazed at the water's edge. Hundreds of swallows skimmed and dipped over the water. Gulls took off from the rocks ahead of him, gliding overhead and reminding him of the St. Lawrence. He thrust his paddle deeper and with long even strokes sent the little boat skimming along as he sang very softly to himself:

"En roulant ma boule roulant

En roulant ma boule."

Landing at the foot of the stillwater at the head of rifts his eye caught the sign of a trail. Pulling his canoe up into the grass, he followed the trail into the woods, upstream about a third of a mile, pushed through alders and, as he expected, came to a small clearing. A gable roofed log camp was there, the bark roof extending out about five feet over the porch and door.

The place was locked but Louie, intuitively, lifted a butter crock on a shelf by the door and, sure enough, there was a key. He unlocked the door and went inside. Dishes were on the table and there were several chairs, one with a narrow upright board for a back and one big one made of rough hemlock boards with a burlap bag of marsh grass for a cushion. The bed had a good supply of quilts and blankets. Two small stoves, a cook stove and a chunk stove, sat next to each other, the little square cast iron chunk stove in a box of sand and burnt matches. On the wall hung an array of frying pans and kettles, and on the floor lay some old shoes and the leg of a hip boot which someone probably figured might come in handy for something sometime. On a wire over the stove dangled a lot of old socks. Old socks in fact were everywhere. Seemingly anywhere Louie looked he saw an old sock. And there was a pair of trousers with one leg gone, probably used to stuff in a broken window-light. Shirt sleeves and legs to underwear were hanging on another wire over the stove, apparently dish-rags and towels. From a rafter overhead part of a sack of flour was suspended by a string and several pieces of crystalized "white tiger" hung from another rafter. He raised the lid of a wash boiler. There was food; cornmeal, rice, tea, coffee, flour, salt, beans. He pawed around on the shelf over the window; Winchester shells, playing cards, tooth picks, a bottle of toothache medicine, an empty flask, a tin box with about eleven old corn cob pipes in it, some yellow pieces of sulphur, the handle of a cross-cut saw, the broken tip of a fish-rod, an old mouth organ, a pair of spectacles, a couple of badly broken cigars, a tin cup with a heavily coated shaving brush in it. Leaning against the wall in a corner were a peavey, an ax and a cross-cut saw. Hanging on the wall were a pair of snow-shoes and fifty or more steel traps.

"Nice warm little camp," he thought, "Good thing to know."

He didn't disturb anything and when he left, snapped the padlock and put the key back under the butter crock.

This camp belonged to Jim McMaster, one of Barber's guides, but it had been built by Kettle Jones, the trapper. Old Kettle Jones—his name was Owen Jones but all Welshmen from the Steuben Hills had handles to their names, though why such a peculiar one in his case isn't apparent—trapped south of the Moose River and West of the Indian and knew the territory intimately. His headquarters was a log camp on Horn Lake, and in all his wanderings he was always looking for gold. Once he took samples of ore out to Hamilton College at Clinton for assay and, when he came back, found that someone had laid out a direct line of blazes on trees between the stillwater and this camp. He became so enraged he never used the camp again. He also claimed that he had a lead mine back in the woods and would take pieces of lead from his pocket and tell how he had cut it out of a vein in a rock. This might have been the same vein that Nichols, Jock Wright's partner, is reported to have discovered before 1800 on a small tributary of the West Canada Creek. Kettle knew too where there was an Indian graveyard near Balsam Lake, for he talked of rows of mounds on flat dry land, one grave right after another. He often declared, "I allus wished I'd took time an' dug up one o' them mounds."

Louie returned to the rifts, knowing now where there was

another camp in the woods and where the trail to it left the big creek. Again shouldering his pack and canoe he went over the carry to the head of another long stillwater. As he paddled on down, rounding the bends, deer trotted across the shoals ahead of him, and he watched their white flags as they leaped gracefully into the cover of the trees. A hawk wheeled high overhead. And heard before it was seen, the slow swish, swish, swish of the broad pinions of a great heron as it made its measured flight across the stream, an ancient looking bird, with looped neck, its little head like a sailor on bow watch, and its long legs and feet trailing astern like a mariner's log-line.

Louie swung around into a new view of the stream and surprised a fox frogging on the shore. The fox took one sharp look at the canoe and made fast time down the narrow strip of gravel at the waterline, never turning to look back a second time. Louie dropped his paddle, raised his rifle and fired. There was a spurt of sand and gravel and the fox disappeared around a point. Slowly lowering his rifle, he blamed the shaky canoe, for shouldn't any fox be a goner once he got him in the sights.

He pushed in to the shore at the foot of the stillwater on the north side and landed between the rocks. The West Creek here dropped over small falls and turned sharply to the south. Near the stream he found a camp which was built like the Wilson Camp at West Canada Lake, a log camp with a bark roof, lean-to style, with a blockade of logs around the fireplace.

He made tea and broiled some meat from his pack. While he slept in the camp that night, deer mice ran over him, hedgehogs waddled about within a few feet of him, weasels looked for fresh venison bones, and out on the stillwater ducks quacked softly, trout jumped and deer splashed at the crossings. Through the sound of running water, through the whisper of the night wind, in the deep dark woods behind the camp a white-throated sparrow sang. Now and then a hoot owl called. On the mountain south of the stillwater a wildcat screamed. It was the same as on the Indian River, on Cedar River Flow, on the Moose, on Sampson Bog.

Next morning Louie reached his destination, Jocks Lake and Barber's place, by going through the woods about two miles over a well-worn trail toward the west. As he was scanning the buildings ahead of him, a large black bear came at him from the side of the trail. Louie jumped back, about to shoot, when a chain fastened to a collar on the bear's neck yanked the bear back just in time.

At Barber's place he was surprised to find such welcome and to be given such good food and drink. Many there had heard Barber tell of his meetings with Louie and real friendliness prevailed. Anyway here millionaire, guide, trapper, gum-picker and lumberjack were treated alike.

Amazia Dutton Barber, a rich man's son, usually called "Dut" or "A.D." first came to Jocks Lake sometime in the early 1880's. He had been sowing too many wild oats in the city and his father had the idea that it wouldn't cost so much to keep him up in the woods. As Jocks Lake was on the large Anson Blake estate and Anson Blake was a friend of the family, Dut, who was really a true lover of the woods, went to Jocks just to look the country over. With him was Rouse B. Maxfield, a friend.

They took the train from Utica to Prospect. The cars were short and light and the upholstery shabby. The roadbed was rough and uneven. Valleys and streams were crossed on open trestles. The train swayed dangerously around the sharp curves, the engine smoke puffing through the open doors and windows, and cinders closed the eyes of many passengers. Riding on the platform of the last car, clinging to the handrail, Dut and Maxfield enjoyed the fragrance of the breezes of the Adirondack foothills.

By previous agreement they were met at the Prospect Station by a team and buckboard and drove on to Wilkinson's, in the woods beyond Nobleboro. Ed Wilkinson's father and mother lived with him and so did his widowed sister and her two children. Dut had no trouble getting accommodations for the night and before retiring made arrangements to team their provisions and luggage to Jocks Lake for ten dollars.

At breakfast they feasted on trout having the flavor that rarely survives transportation from the woods. Soon afterward they started for the lake over nine miles of one of the worst roads in the north. It had been opened for lumbermen and tanners who did most of their hauling in winter when snow made such roads more passable. But the pine and hemlock and much of the spruce had been lumbered off many years before, and though some men from the tannery were still busy with ax and spud, the forest was again returning to its primitive state and the road was sadly neglected. It had become a series of boulders, swamps, mudholes and corduroy patches, yet in spite of the difficulties and the heat and the swarms of flies, they made the trip on foot in three hours. The team arrived at the little grassy clearing at the foot of the lake early in the afternoon, and they camped there that night in a small, bark-roofed, log hut set well away from any large trees that in a high wind might take a fancy to fall.

Before Wilkinson started on his return trip next morning, he let them have one of his boats which he had hidden in the woods and they rowed along the shore finding new beauties in the rocks, trees and waterfalls. Jocks Lake is a crescent of pure water, about four miles long and a mile across the widest part. There are no islands and no swampland along the shore. Landing might be made anywhere but the sandy beaches on both sides of the lower end were choice places for swimming and boating. The hills rose on every side, clad in the somber green of the spruce, but there was no oppressive feeling of silence and isolation that usually belongs to lakes shut in by towering hills. It seemed to be on a plateau and the sensation of altitude was increased by the invigorating atmosphere. Through its crystal waters objects twenty feet below the surface of the lake were visible, the reason for its sometimes being called "Transparent Lake."

They passed Rocky Point where old trapper Jock Wright, a veteran of Bunker Hill, once had his cabin. Back in the year 1796 when fur had become scarce around Lake Champlain, Jock had moved west to the town of Norway, New York. With his partner Nichols, he trapped to the north and became familiar with nearly every source of the East and West Canada Creeks, and on or near a tributary of the West Creek, Nichols "obtained a fine specimen of lead ore." After Nichols died, "Uncle Jock", on one of his wanderings, discovered what was thereafter known as "Jocks Lake". He said it was alive with trout when he first visited it, and for several years he kept its location a secret. He would take loads of trout to the settlements at almost any season. Jock was a man of few words, had a stooping posture and an odd gait, lifting his feet as though treading on something light. When he received a pension from the government, he buried himself still deeper in the woods, hunting and fishing. He died around 1826, aged about seventy-five years.

As Dut Barber and Maxfield explored the shores of Jocks Lake, foxes peered at them and wild ducks sailed past with their young broods. The call of the loon was heard at intervals and they watched them dive and reappear at unexpected places. The woodpeckers hammered on the trees. Early in the morning and toward night they heard the liquid notes of the swamp robin. They landed and prepared to camp. The woods seemed full of owls that hooted all night long. They sat around their fire contented and satisfied that they had found the most beautiful lake in the whole North Woods and as the campfire snapped and blazed and the wild noises of the night wilderness came from the surrounding darkness, Barber decided that on the following day he would choose the site on the thickly wooded shoreline where to build his lodge and play the real host.

They made a temporary camp, a low bark shelter on Rocky Point, on the same site where rotted remains revealed old Jock had had his camp. Then they chose the real site and started "Forest Lodge." Help was brought in from Wilmurt and they rolled up a big log camp for living quarters. Barber's wife, equally in love with the woods, soon joined them.

They made their plans. The following winter Big Eve of Wilmurt had two teams on the road all of the time toting supplies and equipment from Nobleboro and lumber from Richards Brothers' sawmill at Wilmurt. Special flooring was brought in from Utica. The Jocks Lake road in from Nobleboro was all ups and downs. It was said to be uphill either way you traveled it. There were some hard pulls up Town Camp and Thunder Brook Hills and past Whiskey Springs before arriving at Trenton Landing which was across the lake from Barber's. In the winter the teams pulled the sleighloads over the ice but in the summer everything had to be boated across from the landing. A large main camp was built, and four or five two-story cottages, a boat house and stable and a separate building for the guides' sleeping room. The first original log camp became the bar-room.

At the landing a horn was always kept hanging just inside the door of a little horse shed, with which anyone could announce his arrival to the camp on the other side of the lake. Sometimes it might be Charley Wagner coming in on horseback with the mail from Uncle Ed's post office in Wilmurt. When the blast of the horn was heard floating across the water, it didn't take long to get a boat and row across after those newspapers and letters. Or a long toot might mean that Pony Haskell had arrived with a team and buckboard and new guests for the hotel; or it might be Morey Platt, driving for By, with a wagon full of good things to eat. The sound of that horn was surely part of the life at Jocks.

When they were building the place, Mrs. Barber, who once was the little girl that Dut used to swing with on the front gate in

Utica, would appear about ten o'clock in the forenoon with baskets of sandwiches, pastries, delicacies and bottled beer, and all of the work would stop as the men sat around and enjoyed the refreshments. She was a wonderfully nice little woman, and, although she was crippled from falling off that same front gate, she loved to ride horseback, hunt, fish and row on the lake. Barber had a fleet of about thirty boats, all alike with shining nickle trimmings and cane seats. In the hunting season Mrs. Barber would help put out the dogs.

Barber kept open house, gave food, shelter and entertainment without charging a cent. Barber Sr. was a lobbyist at Albany, and through him easy money found its way to his son, enough to keep him contented and satisfied to be away from the attractions of the city. Folding money came by mail and small heavy packages of hard money by express. And also, at the Poland bank, Dut had a checking account with a balance of a few thousand dollars kept in a healthy condition by his father.

Money was so plentiful that the first year or so everything was free, no charge for anything, and Dut had all of his old friends and acquaintances up from Utica. They brought lots of money with them and fancy drinks. Barber bought his liquor from Smith & Brown in Utica; and in the back room were several barrels of fine whiskey, the best, no "scratch all", with spigots on them. Take your choice! Sometimes, on special occasions, under a little rustic roof like a small open summer house, a keg of whiskey with a spigot and a tin cup on a chain was there for those who wanted to help themselves. Lumberjacks, gumpickers, trappers were all welcome. No class distinction at Barber's!

Special guests too were coming, probably on invitation from the old man, from anywhere east of the Mississippi. Barber was running it like a hotel, to all intents an inn keeper, except for the important element of receiving compensation. He had a register and in one year eight hundred people signed; but of course, Dut was a good poker player, and during those first few years, most guests just about had to play poker all night or they didn't stay long.

Barber often won or lost a thousand dollars on the turn

of a card. He lost six thousand dollars on one hand of poker to a sport from Utica. But he was always a game loser. He was friendly, a "prince of a fellow", a "swell guy", and with no exaggeration, a gentleman and a scholar.

Dut and Pony Haskell once played seven-up to see who would sit all day on a rock out in the lake. Pony lost and sat out there all day in the rain. The next time they played to see who would swim to Gull Rock and Barber lost. It was on a freezing cold day in November but Dut swam to the rock, about half a mile, with a boat alongside carrying his clothes.

This good sport was as good at cards as at swimming. There were parties who came in with the idea of trimming him but they always went out broke. Somehow Barber seemed to clean them up one way or another. If they came in with dogs and guns, they went out without them although Barber couldn't do anything fancy with a deck of cards. He dealt the cards straight and played square.

One day, when Pony Haskell was working at Barber's making shingles, he could not believe his eyes when he turned and saw his young son, Trume, a boy around ten, standing beside him.

"What are you doin', boy, way up here in these big woods?" he asked.

"Some mail came for Mister Barber and I fetched it in," Trume told his father. "He give me these."

"Give you what?"

Trume held up a tin cup full of nickels. "Mister Barber give 'em to me."

It took him much longer to return home as he had to stop and rest so often by the side of the road and count those nickels.

When Barber's place was first run as a regular hotel on a business basis in the summer of 1887, most of his early patrons suddenly disappeared. He was charging a regular rate of twelve dollars a week but it was no uncommon thing for him to play a game of seven-up to see if the new arrival would pay nothing or double.

Barber gradually expanded his hotel facilities. On each of the half dozen or so lakes and ponds lying within five or six miles of Jocks Lake, he built comfortable camps outfitted with blankets and cooking utensils and at every camp was a good flat-bottomed boat or even a sixty pound Rushton which was a pleasure to row and not a hard boat to carry.

He had a very attractive booklet printed and distributed, illustrated with many wood-cuts. "Forest Lodge, A. D. Barber, Jr., Proprietor. . . . . the largest, finest, best kept and most popular hotel in this part of the woods . . . . health-giving and strength-restoring resort for invalids and persons in need of rest and quiet . . . . lakes and streams abounding in speckled trout, and mountain fastnesses where the majestic buck, graceful doe and spotted fawn are often found . . . . gentlemanly and well trained guides are furnished for parties wishing to take excursions further into the wilderness. The guides receive $3.00 per day when accompanying parties and furnish their own board . . . . three miles to the northeast of Forest Lodge is a beautiful group of lakes, the first of which is Jones Lake, a pretty little sheet nestling among the mountain peaks like a diamond in a setting of emerald . . . . Moose Lake, one half mile from Otter, is a famous place for deer . . . . At a point on the Jocks Lake road, two miles from the lake, stands a mammoth birch tree with an ax marked and fire blackened bole. Near here a trail leaves for Salmon Lake, famous for the size of its speckled inhabitants . . . . If a person has the time to spare, it cannot be devoted to a better purpose than a trip to the Canada Lakes, a beautiful group, the nearest one, South Lake, being only four miles from the Third or Upper Stillwater. North Canada is reached by a one-half mile carry from South. Blue Mountain Lake can also be visited by this route, making the trip from Jocks Lake in three or four days . . . . First class deer hunting is to be had at Jocks Lake, and during the open season venison is invariably included in the menu at Forest Lodge. Forest Lodge has one of the best pack of deer hounds in the country . . . . Taken all in all, Forest Lodge, at Jocks Lake, is the ideal place to spend a vacation in the North Woods."

One of the woodcuts in the booklet was a picture of forty pounds of brook trout caught by A. B. Gardner in Jones Lake. The fishing was certainly good. "Shady" Groves, clerk and chore-boy for Barber, was rowing the boat for Judge Higley trolling for lake trout. The judge was more interested in the idea of buying a little piece of shoreline than he was in fishing and told Shady to row in and take a look. As they neared the shore to land Shady relieved the judge of the bothersome length of line and started to pull in. There was a real strike and a battle and Shady hauled in what turned out to be a fourteen pound lake trout.

TROUT FISHING ON JONES' LAKE.

An extract from a diary shows how the fishing was at Barber's.

"*June 1, 1888*. Left Prospect 9 A.M. Hired team. Reached State House at North Lake at 3 P.M. Key of Barber's boat on South Lake not to be found. Stayed all night.

June 2. Up early. Caught a half pounder under the flume on bait having tried flies without success. Worked half a mile of Black River. Caught half a dozen small trout. 11 A.M. Giles Becraft reported with party from Barber's for whom my team was sent in. Started for Barber's 1 P.M. It was very cold. Ran 2 miles of South Lake in 18 minutes. The little Rushton on Jocks ran like a deer, made 4½ miles in 32 minutes. Arrived chilled through. A hot stove and a good supper and early to a good bed in a cozy bedroom.

June 3. About 10 A.M. with two others started for Otter Lake. All good trails. Before we had finished dinner rain began. Fished in it a couple of hours and took 20 averaging ¼ lb. on fly.

June 4. Cold morning and foggy on lake. Trout rising splendidly to the fly. Took 11 in 1 hr. when the breakfast summons came, largest ½ lb. The other rods with bait during the evening and morning did rather better than I. After breakfast impatient to try Jones Lake, which had great repute for large fish, returned to it, rest of my party went out. I found a party of 3 from Herkimer and with them fished Jones Lake several times thoroughly during the day. Result 3 trout, one of ½ lb. 2 of about 3 oz. each. Weather grew very cold with strong north wind. The guides went to Deer Lake and returned in 3 or 4 hrs. with about 10 lbs. of nice trout.

June 5. Although ice made in our buckets outside of camp, we had not known that it was so cold for we had found a remarkably comfortable camp with lots of blankets. All of us went to Deer Lake and had a good day's fishing although the wind was so strong and gusty that our boats, unprovided with stern anchors, circled constantly and scared the fish. The flies of all descriptions were faithfully tried but not a single rise did we get to them. We took about 80 trout averaging a good ¼ lb. Returned early to Jones Lake, the wind having gone down and apparently the chance of fishing it better, our evening's fishing on it was blank.

June 6. Another cold night with ice. The temperature at Barber's 26 degrees, but we passed it comfortably. As it bade fair to be a good day 2 of the party remained to fish the lake. I, with a guide and companion, started across the mountain for

66

some rift fishing in the W. Canada Creek. The distance is said to be 2 miles. It seemed much longer. No trail and our route led straight away up a very steep hill and down into a quagmire filled with windfalls. We were 1 hr. and 40 minutes reaching the creek on which we spent the day, moving about 4 miles on the stillwater and fishing a mile of rifts with indifferent success. I took 6 or 8 with fly on the rifts, none in the stillwater, then I went over the same route with bait and took twice as many and larger. The three miles trail back to Barber's is easy and we made it in 30 minutes. Found a very high wind on the Lake and no boats out. About sunset it moderated a bit and I pulled to a rocky point. After trying artificial bait unsuccessfully, put on a big dew worm and it was hardly in the water before I had hold of a trout which gave me the business for ¼ hr. He scaled a little over 2 lbs. Passing a shanty of a camping party from Herkimer, I was shown by one of them a much larger trout than mine taken the day before. It was a good three pounds, and it, with about sixty pounds of smaller ones, was snugly stowed with moss and filled a butter tub. Congratulating the old fellow on his extraordinary good luck for five days' fishing, he said. "Yes, but this is not the half of them."

June 7. A calm bright warm day. Lay around resting up, reading up and getting posted up. Amused myself playing with the hounds, of which a fine pack of 14 friendly fellows are chained to their commodious kennels and all eager for a little petting. Among them are several with records and several of mixed breed. One which is largely blood hound, among the best tempered until a deer is killed then handle with care is the motto. Another, judging by appearance, has far more shepherd than hound blood, yet through his superior intelligence, is considered one of the best. The pet bear also furnished his share of amusement, but best of all were the fishing cats. The pair are large, handsome and spotted. One watches closely at the edge of the pond till a dace or shiner comes within reach when with a quick grab it catches it and permits its mate to eat first. During the day several parties fished unsuccessfully and toward sunset I made a good tryout. Failed to get a strike.

June 8. Learning that a party of ten were expected to arrive at State House by noon, 6 of us started for home to take advantage of return teams and reached Prospect by 7 P. M. without incident.

Summary. In 10 days I traveled about 80 miles by rail, 40 miles on foot, 30 miles in boats, camped out 4 nights, fished 18 hrs. and took 12 lbs. of trout, the largest 2 lbs. There were many hours of suitable weather that were spent in idleness for it did not pay to waste them on either Jocks Lake or Jones Lake, magnificent sheets of trout water, which should have given us all we wanted to do. But the party with the butter tubs was the only one that could get trout out of them. I heard that they had several more tubs and for many years the same party has enjoyed the same success sending out from one tub to a dozen of solid meat trout. Members of the party go out of camp at early daylight, return in a couple of hours with many pounds. They disclaim the use of set-lines, baited traps and gill nets, but before netting and fishing through the ice became illegal during the times when Jocks Lake had no inhabitants on its shores, this party made no secrets as to its methods. Now they claim that the nets which they are known to have are to catch minnows for bait and their buoys for lake trout.

There is no doubt in the mind of anyone who lives in this locality, and little in that of visitors, that Jocks Lake and Jones are being systematically netted and skinned of their trout. Unless some steps are taken to prevent, the time is soon coming when they will cease to be trout lakes.

The game constable I have never met, but common report says that he is too old and infirm to prove a source of danger to those disposed to violate the law. Mr. Barber had made an attempt to restock the lake putting in some 8,000 fry, but he had little hope of success inasmuch as a large portion of the fry furnished him were so very young that many had not as yet got rid of the sack."

Not many women came to Barber's and most of those who did come stayed close to the lodge. A couple of women went over to Jones Lake with Mike Lyons as their guide. Mike, who was an awful man to swear, proved to them on this trip, to their shocking amazement, that fishing required just so much profanity. Every time that Mike swore, which was often, he pulled out a trout, but the women, fishing in the same place, were not catching any at all. They wouldn't swear. Mike would let out an awful curse just as he raised his bait to near the surface where the trout were taking it and out would come a nice one. The women were fishing too deep and they didn't get wise even when Mike borrowed one of their rods to show them that it worked just as well on one rod as it did on another.

Dut had between fifteen and twenty guides, with Frank Baker in charge. Others were Giles Becraft, Andrew Carmen, Eddie Robertson, Fred Kreuzer, Jim McMasters, Mike Lyons, Nat Shepard, Albert Flansburg, John Heirs and the two Hart Brothers. Andy Carmen had come into the woods to die of consumption. He picked the blisters on balsam trunks and licked the juice and "it worked." Instead of being an invalid he became a giant. Most every native in Wilmurt worked for Barber at one time or another. The guides had their own quarters and good old Grandma Clancy from North Wilmurt cooked and waited on them.

At the end of every season there was a grand round-up of all the natives in that section of the woods. The sports had all gone out and every guide, woodsman and teamster, all who could get away from work; hied over the rough roads to Barber's on Jocks for a free time. The town of Wilmurt always turned out about en masse for a free drunk. The bar was wide open. They played cards and ate and drank until morning, and those who lost had to wait on the others. In the morning the dogs were put out.

Sometimes they took the dogs and all the whiskey that they could carry on their backs and went over to Jones Lake for several days. They ate the fore-quarters of the game they got and the saddles they brought out to divide up among them. And they didn't worry themselves about any game laws.

One big hunt was pulled off by the whole party over on the West Creek in which not a deer was killed. The First Stillwater

69

was their destination.   It was barely daylight when some, after being up all night, broke away from their games.   Others were aroused and all made their way to the dining room.   Those sleeping in the cottages stepped out into the half-dark cold still air and with their Winchesters on their arms walked over frost sparkling boards to stow away a substantial breakfast of which venison and flapjacks formed the biggest part.   It was a great hunting morning and the hounds knew that something unusual was going on.   They were yelping at the kennel where as usually they were so patient and quiet.   Guides took care of the hounds, ten of them, "the best pack of deer hounds in the whole North Woods."   They were coupled and straining at their chains as the party started over the trail toward the east, bragging about what they were going to do.

On reaching the First Stillwater the guides listened to last instructions and started for the hills to put out the dogs, and the rest of the party each made for his respective station, some walking, some in boats.   Louie, with two others, took a boat to a good place near the head of the stillwater.   At about eleven o'clock they heard the hounds at a distance followed by several shots but the baying continued for over an hour, growing fainter and fainter and at last ceasing.   They walked around a bit and stretched their legs and then heard the dogs baying again and got back to their posts.   The dogs seemed to be driving the deer right toward them when, splash, and a deer jumped into the water near where Byron Cool was seated on a matting of boughs behind a big rock.   He shot several times but the deer merely shook its head and kept swimming for the other shore. Someone on the other side tried to run and head it off.   He fired two shots at a distance of about fifty yards but the deer . reached the shore and was soon out of sight.   Byron said later that he saw three or four deer, or it might have been only one, run in one side of the stillwater and out the other.   Later all the hunters gathered at the log lean-to at the foot of the stillwater to go back again over the trail to the lodge.   They had the same to report.   The deer, with twenty good men shooting at them had been safe. That day the cream of the hunters of the southern woods went back to Jocks without meat.

Barber's freight came to Prospect railroad station, and it was By Congdon's job to pick it up and take it in as far as Grif Evans' hotel at Nobleboro where it was left for Big Eve to tote it in to the lake. Billy Hughes was a driver for By. Once when Billy came back from over on the Trenton Road, he brought a little bear cub with him that some one had dug out of a den when it was no bigger than a kitten. Billy put the cub upstairs in By's barn, and, chained to a post, the little bear paced back and forth continually, dragging the chain across the floor, until By said, "Better get rid of that bear, Billy. Take 'im up to the lake."

So Billy took the cub to Ed Wilkes' place and handed him over to Big Eve, who took him up to Barber's where the little cub became a full grown bear. Then there was much amusement to be had by those sitting in the back of the hotel right after breakfast where they could see where the tame black bear was kept in a sort of dug-out built of logs and covered over with dirt in a little hill close beside the trail that led over to the First Stillwater. When guests going fishing would pass this spot, the bear came charging out of his hole and ran toward them, just as he had toward Louie, aiming to get into their baskets as he had been taught to look there for food. Newcomers who knew nothing about the bear's den were freightened out of their wits before the bear reached the end of the chain which allowed him to just reach the trail. Louie who began going quite often to Barber's, never tired of watching them.

Baker, the head guide, would rather play and wrestle with the bear than eat, and when business was good at the bar, Dut often told him to fetch it in. The only time they could do much with the bear was when he was about three-quarters drunk. First, Baker gave him a bottle of beer which the bear took hold of with his front paws and drank. Next he gave him a milk punch of a quart of milk and a pint of whiskey. Then they had their fun. Baker led him around and showed him off. He would bring the bear into the

71

main lobby of the hotel where it amused the guests by staggering and rolling on the floor and sucking his feet but when bruin began to sober up they had to watch out and keep a safe distance from those front paws. He was ugly then and Baker did not fool around long before getting him back again into his enclosure.

At one of these exhibitions old bruin did his stunts and all was merry until he started for the storeroom which was next to the bar.

"Don't let that bear in there," the bartender yelled. "Get 'im out o' there."

Louie, who was there at the time, jumped to help. Holding on to the chain about the bear's neck, they were dragged through the doorway into the storeroom. A heavy front paw went into a big cheese as if it were so much pudding. As stuff began to fall more help crowded in until finally the bear was conquered and pulled and pushed back into his little log and earth shelter in the rear.

"He came out of it pretty quick that time, Frank," one of the guides said. "You better double the strength of that milk punch."

"He's growed up."

Even when he was hibernating, they had their fun with him. One February day, Baker and a couple of guides who were wintering there dug him out of his straw bed in the hillside den and hauled him on a hand-sleigh into the barroom where he was aroused from his stupor by having a generous portion of strong drink poured down his throat. But he woke up in a bad mood and the men had to back up to avoid his flailing paws. Before damage was done, they hustled him back into the den where he soon dropped off into the winter's sleep.

Barber had the bear for three or four years. Then a sportsman arriving for the spring fishing missed the bear and asked the bartender what had become of it.

"Say, that old bear got so ugly he had to be done away with. After the sports had left and most of the guides had gone home we killed him. Grandma Clancy had gone home for the winter to North Wilmurt so we had to do the cookin' ourselves. The meat was kind of white like pork because he wasn't running wild but had been fed here off the hotel stuff."

This bartender of Barber's, who was also general handy man around the place, had long hair down to his shoulders, the result of losing a presidential election bet with Dut. If Barber

JOCK'S LAKE, FROM TRENTON LANDING.

had lost he would have had to quit shaving. The bartender was the unlucky one but got to like it, so he left it that way as it helped him in his new hobby of dressing up in a wild west outfit and shooting at targets with a big revolver.

They liked Louie at Barber's and looked out for him. When he left after a visit, Dut usually had one or two of his guides trail him the next day as far as Jones or Poor Lakes or to the Second Stillwater to see that he got through all right. It would probably be Eddie Robertson and Andy Carmen who followed him; anyone but Baker, for in an argument Louie had threatened to shoot him.

Once, after several subzero winter days when almost anyone

73

would have been glad to stay inside, Louie took it into his head to start for home. He put on his snowshoes and they watched him stride off and disappear down the trail toward the First Stillwater.

"How far will he get by dark?"

"Oh, he'll stay at McMaster's camp tonight."

"It's goin' to be a cold night."

"There's wood there and a good stove."

The day was cold and the night colder. "Eight below," one reported. A half hour later "Eleven below." Twelve . . fifteen . . twenty-two. It was a cold night!

"I wonder how Louie's makin' out."

"He's all right."

But Barber didn't know whether he was all right or not. The following morning he had to get it off his mind.

"How about you and Andy trailin' Louie to see that he's all right?" he said to Eddie Robertson.

So Eddie and Andy snowshoed along Louie's trail. They figured that they would go to McMaster's camp on the Second Stillwater and stay there for a couple of hours with a warm fire, get something to eat and then come back. But just before reaching the First Stillwater they came to a sudden stop. Louie's tracks had turned north.

The tracks led to Otter Lake. There Louie had walked up on to a great mound of snow and then burrowed down four or.five feet at one side of it to a small opening in the side logs of the dog-house and crawled inside through the dark hole. He slept on the dry grass that had been the dogs' bed, comfortably warm from the contents of the bottle that he consumed. Then he had moved on, for when the trackers came on to the place there were fresh tracks not over two or three hours old leading away.

"There goes his tracks," Andy said, "straight for Goose and Poor, and I'll bet they go through the notch to Northrup and down the outlet to one of his camps on the Indian. Let's go back an' tell Dut."

The Outside

Chapter Seven

There were two routes in to Barber's Place.

The usual one was by way of Wilmurt. They reached Prospect by train and there took the stage ($1.50 fare) or were met by appointment by By Congdon's spring-seated rigs. One rig loaded up with duffel, the others with men. The destination would be "Uncle Ed" Wilkinson's "Wilmurt House" near the bridge at Wilmurt or at Grif Evans' big hotel in Nobleboro. Changing to buckboard drawn by one of Big Eve's teams, they went at a cost of $6 or $8 some five hours and thirteen miles farther to Jocks Lake. On that lap of the journey a buckboard was the only conveyance suitable for carrying human beings without shaking the daylights out of them. Even so, "those who rode wished they had walked, though those who walked wished they had rode."

Uncle Ed Wilkinson—his full name was John Edward

Spencer Wilkinson but all called him Wilks or Uncle Ed Wilks —was a genuine native of the North Woods.

His grandfather, Francis Wilkinson, who was born in England in 1792 and arrived in this country as a boy of eight, was a pioneer settler in the locality. He bought land in 1824 from Arthur Noble, land proprietor who projected a great city, and he settled on the West Canada Creek some three miles above the Forks, where on a promontory between the East and West Branches there had been erected in the 1770's a frontier post, consisting of earthwall and palisades, call Fort Noble. Francis built his house and planned a gristmill at the nearby falls. Heavy millstones were purchased in Albany. It took three months and cost $28, a respectable sum in those days, for an ox team to bring them in. But the Wild West Creek wouldn't be harnessed, the dam wouldn't hold, the stones were never used. They still lie, embedded in leaves and dirt, at the proposed site of the mill.

Noble himself had better luck with a sawmill, which earned him some international fame. For the report is, "Arthur Noble built the first sawmill in Herkimer County in 1790. The first lot of lumber sawed in the mill was shipped to Ireland. He rafted it down the West Canada Creek, thence down the Mohawk to Cohoes Falls, then carted it to the Hudson at Albany, where it was loaded on sloops for the Old Country" . . . which was indeed quite a feat if he did it. One wonders how he got past Prospect and Trenton Falls and the Gorge.

It was at his grandfather's place, "the last house in civilization," that Uncle Ed was born and grew up, then later moving to Wilmurt where he maintained "The Wilmurt House," on the best corner in Remsenburgh Patent which had been bought from Noble.

Uncle Ed was a congenial, neighborly old man, well liked, and set a good table. Dut Barber, in his hotel booklet, advised his guests to stop there on their way in and get a square meal, a meal that probably would be a slice of ham and about half a dozen eggs with the fixings or maybe venison or brooktrout for twenty-five cents.

Uncle Ed also ran a little store with a few groceries, kept a boarder or two, and had the post office for the town of Wilmurt. He was an assessor and had been supervisor and town clerk. His able housekeeper weighed two hundred and twenty-five pounds but she could handle herself and the lumberjacks too and keep order. "Rather see her and Dave Dolan dance than anyone else, both big and light on their feet," one fellow said of her. A hunter, who had stopped for dinner, remarked, "I'd hate to hafta keep her in meat."

In the store part, Uncle Ed had a narrow counter, which served as a bar, and back of it a tall ice-box in which he kept the brown pitcher of beer that was familiar to so many. If there was any left after filling the customers' glasses, the pitcher went back again into the ice-box to await the next customer, until Uncle Ed would have to go down cellar to refill it.

UTICA SATURDAY GLOBE,

A Popular Haunt of Old-Time Uticans

Ed Wilkinson's hotel, The Wilmurt House, at the gateway to the Adirondacks,

Ed Wilkinson, of Wilmurt, Herkimer County. What of it? Nothing; only ask some of the old timers of Utica WHAT about it, and they'll give you full information right off the reel. They'll tell you that this old "tavern" was famous during the Civil War and before. Aye! long before Saranac was on the map, or Camp Dart or any other of the well-known summer resorts in the Adirondacks were dreamed of. Ed in his day was the best-known guide in the North Woods and later on served time as a supervisor for the town of Wilmurt and made and unmade laws at Herkimer. But after a spell, as his whiskers whitened more and more and his locks grew thinner and thinner, Ed eased up a bit and got him an easy chair, settled down in this tavern as you now see it to attend to all who came his way and wanted his goods, bar none. "Bar" sounds a bit spiffy,

I will agree. But there are many genial souls in Utica yet who will smile when they read this, also long for a smile over Ed's old bar—what? Honestly, folks, it was a fine old stopping place before you wandered into the nearby wilderness where the bears, the trout, the deers and other alluring creatures of the Adirondacks awaited you. Ed was partial to Uticans, and for a long time ahead of season his tavern was sold out to guests from Pent Up exclusiyely. If I should mention the names of just a half dozen of Ute's best and most favorably-known citizens who had "eased down" a bit in this famous tavern you'd read the names of men who helped make the nation's history. Ed Wilkinson's old tavern didn't look much outwardly. But inwardly—and what was there to be found, tasted or sniffed—oh, well! What's the use!

He had a liquor license hanging in his cobwebby window, a perfectly good license framed with a glass on it. It had been hanging there for over five years and was just as good as ever.

77

The "Billy Raines man," came through now and then and it was generally believed that he was out to get old Ed or Pony Haskell or one of the many bars above the Flansburg Bridge for some liquor law violation, but he always sent post cards, at least to Ed and Pony, a week or so ahead, saying that he was coming up to look them over.

The other route to Barber's was a twenty-four-mile drive from Prospect to the State House on North Lake. The charge for this was four dollars for a horse and buggy and seven or eight dollars for a team. It was two miles farther over a worse road to South Lake, then a mile and half of trail and a four mile row on Jocks brought the party to Barber's.

Once, in early summer, Louie, going out of the woods from Jocks, walked into Byron Cool's little eight-by-ten barroom at the end of the North Lake dam and dropped his pack by the door.

"Hello, Louie," Byron set up a glass and bottle on the plain board bar.

Two weather beaten cronies, lanky guide George Wandover and Stubby Kettle Jones, the trapper, were sitting on the bench across the end of the little room.

"French Louie," George whispered to Kettle, "He's got a bearskin in his pack there."

"Yeah. Gosh, George, I've killed more bear than he ever saw." Then louder to Louie, "Be yo' goin' out, Louie?"

"Mebbe," Louie answered, "Mebbe so."

"The last time I see you, Louie, was back on the Indian. You never knowed I was there."

Louie poured himself another drink and turned and looked at Kettle Jones. "You don' tink ol' Louie see. You work on dugout canoe dere. You have wan beeg fight wid de mout' wid 'noder mans. You bod tak oup ax an' chop heem all oup Ol' Louie he was be dere."

"Who was it, Kettle?" Wandover asked. "You and Duane Tanner?"

78

"Waal, what of it. 'Twarn't so bad as when you shot ol' Taylor's bull."

"I'd been bird huntin'." George came back at Kettle. "I run out of sixes an' slipped in a couple of BBs thinkin' I might see a fox."

"Yo' didn't have to go an' shoot a man's bull."

"Th' bull was a comin' stret at me. What was I gonna do? I stood my ground an' give 'im th' right behind th' shoulder."

"I heared all that before."

"Anyhow, Kettle, when ol' Taylor goes to get his bull that night, he fetched 'im back on a stone-boat."

"Still and all George, there's no call to go shootin' a man's bull."

Louie stood by the window overlooking the lake, his narrow eyes searching the opposite shore, resting for a moment on some black scarred stump or grayish rock or on a boat tied up to a dock of a hidden camp, paying no attention to the two old trappers behind him.

"But you went floatin' an' shot the jack-staff clean off," George reminded Kettle. "Over on South Lake. The jack fell in the lake an' left you in pitch blackness with no deer. That's darn good huntin', Kettle."

"Why consarn you, what in tarnation's come over yo'? Who went an' told you a thing like that?"

"Atwell Martin told me."

"He blabbered that?"

Guide Giles Becraft with an outwardbound party from Barber's stopped in to say hello to Byron, and Louie learned that there would be room for him on the buckboard that was to take them out. He picked up his pack and followed the others across the dam to the State House where the buckboard was waiting for them.

"Louie here's a goin' out," Becraft tells the driver. "Got room for 'im somewheres?"

"Sure, up with me thar on the front seat," the driver says as he pulls on the ropes and securely ties the packs on the back end and then he climbs up with Louie.

"Get up you. Come on, boy."

Over the bridge at the outlet, past the little clearing at the foot of the lake where old hermit Atwell Martin lived. And there, ahead of them, coming toward them on the road, was as odd a sight as anyone ever saw in the whole north woods. Atwell himself was coming up the middle of the road with his cane and wearing a pair of his own homemade pants which looked as though they had been made out of an old rag rug. He moved to the side to let the buckboard by.

"That's old Atwell," the driver said, and Louie listened to stories about Atwell Martin all the way to Reed's Mills.

"He come in here on account of some love affair he had on the outside where he lived in a log house on the woods' side of Baker Brook near Remsen. He come in here to North Lake and lived in the state barn while he was a buildin' that wigwam o' his. Atwell picked up some money at guidin' in a small way. They say he's got his name in a book that was printed down to Saratogy called 'Guides to the Wilderness'.

"Gosh, he got the job tendin' the state dams. He tended three of 'em, the North Lake dam here, Twin Lakes an' up on Canachagala. He made good money an' lived in the State House, but he went back to his wigwam again. He lost all of his money one way or 'nother, lending it to people mostly.

"Superstitious too. Gosh, yo' know he's got a dried out carcass of a skinned weasel ahangin' over 'is door to keep the witches away. And eat, boy, how he can eat, sometimes! He can eat more than any ten men in the woods. He can live for a time on nothin' an' then fill up when he gets a chance. Once, at Cool's, he set down to a table where there was a big pan of apples and—steady boy, pick up your feet—an' he et the whole darn panful.

" 'Did yo' have enough,' " Byron asked him.

" 'Wall, I guess I made out a mess'," Atwell said.

"Gosh, he never had much more'n a little injin meal an' a

piece o' pork in his wigwam. Once, he wasn't feelin' good an' he et five quarts of wild raspberries right down to cure his ailment. Gee you, Jerry, steady, Mollie. Yeah, Old Atwell was a queer old duck. There was a summer sport up here last year an' he had 'is wife with 'im. He'd knowed Atwell for a long time, years back, an' he wanted his wife to meet the old fellow. So one day Atwell comes along by the State House where the sport was a settin' on the piazza with his wife. 'Mister Martin,' he calls out to Atwell, 'this is my wife.' 'I s'pose so,' Martin says an' keeps right on walkin'.

"He was fussy, Atwell was, an' quick to find fault with the way others did things but gosh he was all right. The law breakers liked Atwell because his word was good an' they knew that no one could nail him up to a tree an' make him tell on anyone.

"I hear tell how his brother Obediah was in with him once for a few days. Old Martin give this brother five dollars to go to Forestport to get out some groceries, but with the scare of hearing about the great sea serpent in the Forestport pond Obediah forgot all about Atwell's foodstuff. The town was all excitement. Two men had come runnin' in yellin' about this old water monster they saw rise up in the pond. In broad daylight too. That night all the villagers who were brave enough gathered together and watched with bonfires blazing along the shore. And, you know, that old sea serpent, he came up and showed himself again. Crowds saw him and then in a few seconds he went down out o' sight in a big whirlpool. Some people say it was just a big bunch of sawdust that got gas in it, but by golly, them that saw it ought to know. Old Punkeyville got something to remember that time.* Here we are at Reeds, Louie, be a good fellow an' open that gate?"

Louie jumped down off the seat and swung open the bars across the road ahead of him, the bars that Reed had on each side of his property to keep his cattle from straying. The stage moved slowly through and waited for Louie to close the bars, then on past Reed's house and barns. One could see the roof of the sawmill back of the house, down on the Black River at the falls. This was one

---

* Serpent story as told in "Snubbing Posts" by Thomas C. O'Donnell.

81

of the last "up and down" power saws in the woods. "Up one day and down the next" as an old timer said.

After Louie opened and closed the second set of bars, they crossed the bridge over the Black River and went on down the other side past Pony Bob Roberts' and about four hours later pulled into Prospect in time for the night train south. Louie took the train to Utica. Sometimes on these woods trains, the smoking car full of lumberjacks was "all hell let loose," so rough, in fact, that when the conductor, coming through to take the tickets, took one look in the car door at the wild commotion inside, the swinging arms and legs in the blue air, he would step back and say, "By Gawd, I'm not goin' in there."

The reason for Louie's trip out of the woods dated back to the spring. When the fishermen were at the West Canada camp, Fred Ralph of Utica had said to him, "When you come down to the city, bring down the bear skins. I know some people who would buy them."

So after Louie had sold his jerked venison at the Bagg's Hotel he trod over the hard stone sidewalks to the office of Fred Ralph, the brewer. Ralph was glad to see him and called a few friends on the phone, and that evening Louie was entertained at the exclusive Fort Schuyler Club. Many of them at the club had been on fishing trips to the West Canada Lakes and this meeting was more of a treat for them than it was for Louie. Louie showed his bearskin and easily turned it into money.

In the forenoon of the next day Fred Ralph had a phone call from the police station. "We've got a drunken woodsman locked up down here, Mister Ralph, who says he knows you. He got into a fight last night at the canal barns and hit a fellow over the head with a shovel and near killed him. He says his name is French Louie."

Ralph called Tom Parker, another of the West Canada fishermen, and through their influence Louie was released and started north.

Across the hot shining rails of the fifteen New York Central tracks through smoke and cinders, and over the Mohawk River

82

bridge to North Genesee Street, past many swinging doors on the river flats, past Deerfield Corners, Louie strode towards the hills and away from the smells of the city.

Getting into his woods gait, with his pack on his back, he jogged along the country road where cows gazed at him from the pasture fences and dogs ran barking from the houses. At the foot of the big hill he turned from the turnpike onto the somewhat easier grade of the plank road and trudged slowly up to the top where, through the trees, he looked back at the blanket of smoke lying low over the crowded mass of chimneys and buildings below him. He faced to the north and ahead of him, the far blue undulating second range of hills lifted him to a lighter tread. Those old mountains were waiting for him. Down the winding road he went, through the woods to the old Forest House, where a farmer, after his regular stop for refreshment on his way home from the city, was just climbing into a Democrat wagon. Louie asked for a ride.

"Throw your pack in the back." The farmer knew in his own mind that all woodsmen were lousy and full of woodticks, but he told Louie to get up onto the seat beside him.

Not much was said, the farmer just clucking to his horses and spitting a brown stream over the wagon wheel. "What's Hinckley and Ballou doin' up there now?"

"Dey got plaintee lumberjob," Louie answered.

"You work in the woods?"

"Ah don' work me."

Louie was just another going back to the woods after losing his money in the big city. The team turned in at a farmhouse driveway. "This 's far as I go," the farmer said.

Louie walked past the South Trenton toll gate through the rolling farm lands toward Prospect.

At the Prospect Station the horses and the long Welsh wagons, the buckboards and spring seaters, were getting ready to take their loads north. The pack-baskets and trunks and piles of freight were to be taken by stage to Wilmurt, Morehouseville and in to Barber's place on Jocks. A busy place, this Prospect Station, around train time. Woods business. And there was Billy

Hughes and Morey Platt, By Congdon's drivers. Louie knew Billy. Billy was tightening up his ropes on his load of freight which was all ready to pull out for Jocks. Sure, of course, there was room for Louie.

Through Prospect village and over the plank toll-road to Gang Mills where the logs from the woods were sawed into lumber. The mill here had fifty-two gang saws, so Billy said. "The logs are slabbed first on circular saws," Billy told Louie, "then they're lined up four abreast an' decked two or three high. Some feller pulls the lever an' in they go, shrieking into them gang saws. The whole mill shakes. Yo' know, Louie, up in the rafters, I was up there once when it shook two feet. One night they cut 145,000 board feet. They had their first gang saw here, they tell me, way back in 1848 an' they're still goin' strong. All the lower West Crik is cut off now. Hinkley & Ballou has camps as far up as the mouth of the Indian and it's the second cut from the Seabury Stillwater down. They'll be cuttin' them spruce up your way next. It won't be long now, Louie, before they'll be gettin' up in there."

"Every time I go over this hill," Billy said as the horses climbed the hill outside of Grant, "I can't help but think o' that drunken lumberjack who lived in Prospect but never got home, that is, not for years. His own family hardly knew 'im. He'd stop in all the barrooms along the road an' before he got anywheres near home his roll would be gone, and then he'd be so darned ashamed of himself he'd turn around an' go back again into the woods. But once, by jiminy, he made it. Them who saw 'im go through this here town o' Grant here wondered where the fire was or who was a chasin' 'im. He got home all right. His own wife 'n kids an' all the neighbors, the whole darn town wanted to know how he made it.

"'Say,' he told them, 'when I got atop that hill t'other side o' Grant, I took my hat off an' I just run an' I got here'."

The heavy wagon creaked and sloughed in the ruts and dropped noisily off the stones. "Th' last I heard of 'im he took the Gold-cure down to Whitesboro." The horses pulled evenly and required but little attention. Through Pardeyville Corners,

84

taking the short cut over Stormy Hill and through Cumming's Woods.

Billy told Louie all about the black bear that eventually reached Barber's. "I fetched 'im back when he was no bigger 'n a kitten, an' put 'im up in By's barn. Now you ought to see 'im."

Bill Wright's was as far as Louie rode as Billy would only be going another quarter of a mile or so anyway, as far as Uncle Ed Wilks', where he unloaded. One could see Uncle Ed's place from Wright's. Big Eve would haul the stuff the rest of the way over the woods road. Bill Wright had a regular bar for lumberjacks but Uncle Ed only had a little counter so Louie got off at Wright's.

Several teams were tied outside. One was a typical tin pedlar's rig, well outfitted for carrying and displaying his wares. Louie went into the barroom. Dut Barber was there and a poker game was going on, and, of course, wherever Dut Barber showed up things began to stir. Frank Baker, his head guide, was with him and several others. The pedlar, a little short Welshman from Grant, had joined the game and lost everything. Barber had won the whole lot, the pedlar's money, the horse and wagon, old rags and metals, tinware, clothing, boots and shoes, and he put it all in the poker game.

"Oh, my gosh! Oh, my gosh," the pedlar cried. "My wife will kill me." He cried and wrung his hands until Barber could not listen to him any longer.

"Shut up, will yo'. You get on my nerves. Take your horse and what's left and get out o' here."

Barber, with his friends, often stopped in at the different bars along the road, where the liquor was not of the best quality and asked the man behind the bar sort of jokingly, "What have you got to drink?" The answer might be, "Oh, the kind I drink." Then Barber would say, "Give me anything else but what you drink," and he'd take a bottle out of his grip or out of his pocket and put it on the bar for all those with him and pay the shot.

Louie walked up the road. He didn't see anyone around Uncle Ed's place so he kept right on going through Nobleboro and in on the Jocks Lake road to the old Wilkinson Place, now Pony Haskell's. Different ones had lived at the old place since Ed Wilkinson had moved out to the main road to run the Wilmurt House, but the old house had remained mostly unchanged except for the outside stairway which had been built to lead up to the "Ram's Pasture", as it was called by Pony Haskell, a place to put the lumberjacks and woodsmen who had imbibed a little too deeply. People going in to Barber's would be pleased when they saw Pony, who drove for Big Eve, was going to take them in. Those wanting information on lot numbers and lot lines would go to him too, as he knew more about such things than any man on the creek. He was a good man to know. Right next to the old place Pony had put up another building, a hotel and bar.

Louie stayed at Haskell's that night, and the next morning he and Pony Haskell's young son, Trume, started for West Canada Lakes. Trume thought Louie was about perfect and nothing pleased him more than to go in with Louie and stay a few days at the camp. They left the Haskell Place at six o'clock in the morning with a light pack of five loaves of bread, some butter, a slab of bacon and a ham, about thirty-five pounds. Trume, only a boy but a husky lad and ambitious, carried the pack all the way and it was Louie who carried the fish rods and tackle. Trume knew that if Louie once got the pack on his back, he would not give it up.

Louie's gait in the woods was a good stiff jog of about three miles an hour. It was a peculiar gait as was that of many backwoodsmen; he walked just like a bear in the way he planked his feet down. He was very sure footed and would put a sweat on anyone who had the lucky privilege of following at his heels.

Louie and Trume went up the West Creek to the foot of the First Stillwater, then north past the small lakes and from here they followed the West Creek Range right to Louie's camp, arriving there just before sundown, a distance of between twenty-five and thirty miles.

Home! Louie opened the door and it smelled good. Good to be back, back again to safer surroundings. Back once more to the old familiar mountains and their ways.

A New Camp on Big West

Chapter Eight

Although Louie brought hundreds of hides out to Newton Corners, traded or sold them at the stores and hotels or left them to be sold to the buyer from Gloversville, deer were nevertheless hard to get in many communities. At one time some years before this, they became so scarce around Newton Corners that the natives had to go as far as Big Indian Clearing to get meat for their families.

And there arose much heated controversy about the hounding and jacking of deer. "If you want twenty-five deer" an old guide said to the head of a hunting party, "you might float for 'em and have good luck; you might stillhunt but you would run a good many chances. Give me the dogs and we'll do it."

It was the beginning of conservation and laws were made and repealed. The Curtis Hounding Law, passed at Albany in the winter of 1884-85 was called, by most hotel keepers, the crowning act for the preservation of deer in the Adirondacks. Chas.

Fenton, hotel keeper of Number Four, said, "I rejoice that this fall I shall not be compelled to report the bloody record of the wholesale slaughter of deer by hounding." But when fall came the slaughter was worse than ever. Little attention was paid to the law and hotel man Fenton was threatened with boycott by guides and hunters. Some hotel keepers on the other hand, even bought off game protectors so their guests could club hounded deer.

State game protector Brinckerhoff said that five hundred deer were killed between Beaver River and Morehouseville. A party of four Pennsylvanians camped on the West Canada Creek where the Metcalf comes in. They had a large pointer dog and killed over fifty deer all of which were shipped to market.

Most guides and hunters did as they pleased regardless of the law but the press was against them. One paper printed this.

CUT THIS OUT

Put it on a blank, obtain signatures and send it to your member of assembly.

A Petition for the Protection of Adirondack Deer, for the honorable, the Legislature of New York:

We, the undersigned, residents of_____County, respectfully petition that the law (Chap. 557, laws of 1885) which makes it "unlawful to pursue any wild deer in this state with any dog or bitch" may not be amended in any way as to permit the use of dogs for hunting deer at any time.

(Signed) ._____

In 1886 the first bag limit of three deer per person was enacted but in April, the anti-hounding law was repealed and the press shouted, "The Water Butcher Wins. The Dogs are Loose Again" and a law was introduced providing a penalty of one hundred dollars for jack hunting. The law also read, "no person shall hunt, kill or take alive, any wild deer by the process or mode commonly known as crusting, or enter any place where wild deer are yarded with intent to kill, take alive or destroy the same at any time." Stop market hunting! Stop hounding! Stop jacking! It was one thing to make laws and another thing to enforce them.

Two law-abiding citizens, for there were a few of them, returned to Ed Wilkinson's place to get a foot rule to make sure that they didn't take any undersized trout. "You__you", an old fellow there said to them. He stuttered a little, "You don't want a f__ f__f__foot rule, you want a f__f_,f_,f__fryin' pan."

As to trout. The laws of the state had for some years forbidden the "killing" of trout under six inches in length, but for some reason this clause was omitted in an amendment that was put through in the winter of 1886. One man staying at Grif Evans' in Nobleboro came out with fifty-seven pounds of trout and not one of them was over seven inches. Another had thirteen pounds of the same kind. Creels full of "babies" were shown exultantly. New York did have a law but "the stupid politicians in the legislature did away with it" and as a result bushels of little trout taken from the headwaters of streams were shipped to New York, Philadelphia and Boston markets.

But there were many hotel keepers and guides who did believe strongly in conservation, and of the sports who were coming into the woods, more than a few of them were being awakened to the need of good conservation laws and their enforcement. Lumbermen and most clubs were against a state-owned preserve, but a few far-sighted citizens first, and then the law-makers, were beginning to appreciate the real value of these great North Woods and to see that something had to be done to save them from being destroyed. The nucleus of the Forest Preserve was actually created in 1885 when over 700,000 acres of land was acquired by the state at tax sales.

Even when the game laws were enforced, it was possible for the natives to have their venison or "mountain lamb" in season and out. It was Louie's quick wit which in fact saved Sandy from the consequences.

Sitting in Sandy's kitchen, he sampled a plate of venison.

"T'aint mus'rat," he said licking his fingers.

"Nope," Sandy replied.

"T'aint coon."

"Nope."

"Ba cripe, ah t'ink she's hedgehog."

"I got some veal too, Louie, but me an' you, we eat mountain lamb." Sandy was looking out the front window. "By mighty," he said, "who's that comin'?"

A stranger was coming up the muddy road, into the little clearing, driving a sway-backed horse and riding high, perched up on the seat of an end-spring buggy. He tied his horse to the butternut tree and came toward the house, stomped and scraped the mud off his boots at the end of the step and came in.

"Howdy," he said to Sandy. "What you serving for dinner?"

"How would you like some real nice mountain lamb?"

The man smiled and rubbed his hands together. "That'll just suit me fine."

The newcomer saw Louie in the kitchen. "What are you doin' way out here, Louie?"

"W'at for ah tol' you," Louie answered hardly looking up from his plate.

The man was served in the front room and when finished he mopped off his plate with a piece of bread. "That's good meat," he said. "Have you got some to sell?"

"Sure," Sandy told him.

"Sell me four or five pounds, will you?"

Louie jumped up. "Ah get da meat, Sandy."

"Sit down." But Louie was on his way out into the back room. He knew where the meat was kept.

Sandy heard the meat-saw in the back and soon Louie came in with a chunk of meat and handed it to Sandy. "Five dollaire," he said softly.

Sandy put the meat on a piece of paper and, hesitatingly, gave it to the man, telling him the price.

"What? Well, if that's what it is," the man said and paid Sandy a five-dollar bill.

They watched him drive away.

"Ba da holy feesch!" Louie said. "Good ting for you she was veal."

"Veal?"

"Ba cripe, Sandy, de law man mos' catch you dat tam, ba gosh. He mos' cos' you hunderd dollaire."

In the fall of 1885, the year the hounding law was passed at Albany, Louie packed in more hens until he had twenty-five or thirty and began to build a new camp at the old clearing, a big one on the lakeshore, as good or better than the camp he had at Pillsbury.

Now that he had a real flock of hens, Louie dried venison and packed it in bags, and fed them a hash of ground venison, bones, cornmeal and potatoes. He made nearly the same hash for himself, compounded of venison, potatoes, onions and seasoning which was packed in earthen crocks, covered with hot tallow and kept in the ice hole or in the spring till needed.

The new camp was well situated. Here and there, all around the shore line he picked the straight spruce that he would cut and tow to the clearing about the first of June when the bark would peel. There were not many pines in the West Canada section, just a few scattered around. One big one stood at the outlet of Brook Trout Lake and there were two or three at the Cedars. There were very few hemlocks, the altitude being too high for them, but Louie found enough hemlock and pine to split out what shakes he needed for his roof.

He made a windlass with which to haul the logs out of the water and up to where he would have his camp. He split and shaved planks for his floors.

In June he cut the trees and towed the logs to his landing, rigged up his windlass and a track for the logs to slide on, and hauled them out of the water. Most of the trees were cut on the farther side of the lake. Louie would stand on the larger logs and paddle them across. Once he fell off but when he came up he was near enough to climb on to the log again.

The space was cleared, the foundation stones set and the first of the logs skidded into place when he was warned by the owners of the land, and he held up on the building after the logs had been hoisted up three or four high. This beginning of the camp stood untouched, soon overgrown and hidden by brush and briars, while Louie lived in the old shack at the back of the clearing and at his Pillsbury camp.

A few miles to the east, on the Cedar River, where the Union Bag was operating, the boss of the lumbercamp had been told by the superintendent, Isaac Kenwell, that whenever Louie Seymour showed up, he was to be given anything he wanted, such as pork, flour and beans. "If Louie comes in, treat him right."

During the cold winter months Louie went to this camp often and was well taken care of. Late in the winter, those at the lumbercamp saw him coming in pulling a sleigh with a couple of baskets on it. He came to the cook-house door and unloaded nearly a bushel of eggs.

"My gosh," the boss cook said, "how much? How much do I owe you for the eggs, Louie?"

Louie answered, "No monee for flour. No monee for pork. No monee for bean," and then added with the same old twinkle in his eye, "No monee for egg."

But there was one thing that Louie did want. There was a good kitchen stove out in the settlements that he could buy, and he asked the boss of the camp, if sometime, when he had a tote-team coming in, he would fetch in the stove. "Sure thing," the boss said, "the first time they're comin' in when they haven't got much of a load I'll have 'em put it on for you."

A few weeks later Louie learned that the stove had been toted in. When March crusts came hard and strong, and he could travel without snowshoes, although he carried them with him, he went to the lumbercamp with his sled. All the loose parts of the stove he put into gunnysacks and early in the morning before daylight when the crust was best, he loaded his sled with the parts, got into his harness and pulled away. He reached West Canada before the crust had softened and the next day went back for the rest of the stove. The crust was strong. The pulling was easy on the even grades but pretty tough on the mounds and hummocks. But he got the stove to his camp, the first real cookstove that anyone had ever had in there.

After a year or two the objection of the land owners to Louie's building operations died away. They had heard of his remarks, "Ah used to put out a lot o' fire. Now ah guess maybe ah let 'em burn." The old squatter, in fact was an asset and not a liability. So Louie resumed the erecting of his new camp.

He went to the Corners for rope and gear. At the bar of Osborn's Adirondack House Louie accused Johnny Leaf, the Indian, of stealing traps. Johnny pulled his knife and went at Louie. Louie knocked him down and picked up a big brown cuspidor and threw it hitting Johnny on the head and the tobacco juice spattered all over Johnny's face. Those at the bar jumped between them and were quick to get Johnny outside before someone got really hurt.

Back at the lake again and anxious to get going he laid skids slanting up on to the old logs and added new bright peeled logs to those blackened original ones. A difference in the logs always showed. With the aid of ropes he rolled the logs up the skids and notched the square hewed corners and fitted them in place. The camp grew to two stories with a small third floor in the peak.

Woodsmen and guides with parties came by, stopped and talked with Louie and gave him a hand for a few hours. One who showed up was young Trume Haskell. Trume liked to watch the way Louie did things for Louie did have certain interesting ways of his own in doing little things. Trume was about eighteen years old, a good still hunter, a young man who knew how to take care of himself in the woods. He did not stay long at Louie's but was usually away the next day looking over new country.

Working steadily from sun-up to sunset, Louie brought the new camp to completion. At the end facing the lake he built a seven foot porch extending across the full width. The roof of the camp was steep pitched with practically no overhang and was roofed with heavy shakes. From the porch the door opened into a large room, and in the back corner was a small room, Louie's kitchen, with a back door. All floors and partitions were made of hand split planks about two inches thick. The floor planks were about four or five feet long.

A ladder against the wall led to the second floor, where, on one side, eight or ten men could sleep separated from each other by small logs on the floor. On the other side of the room were three bunks, crossways, with birchbark on a frame between them. The bunks contained loose beaver meadow hay or balsam boughs until Louie began collecting ticking and blankets from the lumber-camps.

The small third floor, up in the peak, was the place where the guides slept when all other available space was taken by the sports.

Louie's part was the kitchen, where he lived, ate and slept. His bunk was like a saw-buck with a canvas between and a blanket over some boughs or hay. He usually slept with his clothes on, just taking off his shoes. The stove was in the middle of the room within easy reach of the bunk. The pancake griddle and his little tea-pail and the can of bear-lard were on the back of the stove, handy. Everything was right at hand including the kindling, so that in the morning he could sit up, swing around, sit on his bunk and start his fire. He would get his little tea-pail going, cut up some potatoes in the bear-lard in the frying pan and with a few pancakes and bearpork he had enough for a satisfying breakfast. He ate with his fingers from the frying pan on the hearthshelf of the stove or with his tin plate on his lap. He could almost get his meal and eat it without getting off of his bunk. Venison would be just warmed through; he would eat it nearly raw with the blood running down his chin. Many times he actually ate it raw, just sprinkling on a little salt. The kitchen very soon took on the look of having been lived in for many years.

And he even had an ice house, or rather an "ice hole." It

was a deep square hole in the ground and he lined the sides with poles and split balsam. This he would fill with the late March sugar-snow, and tramp it down hard. The wet snow would freeze and in the warm days of summer the ice hole would be kept under a blanket of spruce boughs. Here was a place for the fishermen to put their trout, but no one was ever allowed to take ice out of it.

He built a log woodshed about eight feet square next to the main building, and, in rambling style, added a hen-house made like a fort with eight and ten inch logs. The chicken yard was of upright poles and split rails sticking fifteen or twenty feet up in the air. Off to one side he built a crude smoke-house for jerking venison and smoking "salmon." The woodshed roof was nearly flat, while the hen-house roof was a sharp-pitched gable, shingled with wide neatly split boards nearly four feet long. The doors were of heavy split planks.

A few trees were left standing between the camp and the lakeshore, a distance of about a hundred feet. The lower limbs and underbrush were cleaned out, and from the porch there was a view of the mountains across the lake, one of the highest lakes in the Northwoods.

More outsiders kept coming in. It was about this time that guide John Heirs and M. S. Northrup, from Johnstown, went to a little pond west of Brook Trout Lake, caught an incredible mess of beautiful trout and named the pond "Northrup". Heirs said that "this pond had so many fish in it that they ate one another and if you caught one and ate it, it tasted fishy." There was another little lake called Poor Lake where the fishing probably was just that. All over the woods, the sports were following the trails of the old trappers and hunters, and the little ponds way back in were being rediscovered and renamed.

Louie now yoked in new boats from Newton Corners. He always had his eyes open for more boats, for he had them on every lake and stillwater from the Indian to the Cedars and from Sampson to the Moose River. Some of the boats had oars, some had paddles and yoke, and all oars and paddles had handles chewed by hedgehogs. Some were guide boats that he had bought from Buyce, out to the Corners, yoked in in summer or dragged in in winter. Some were sturdy, well-made, round bottom boats, rowed and toted up the West Creek; these had been given to him by the owners of the Oneida Camp at the head of the lake, who were boat builders by trade. Some were crude, flat bottom, square end affairs. Some were light weight cranky little boats that would just about float two men. Some Louie had "found" and yoked far back to some hidden wild stillwater. At one time he had thirty-eight boats, and, except those near the West Canada camp, which were the heaviest, they were pretty well hidden, some nearly a quarter of a mile from water like the one he slept in at his sugar-bush camp.

Roc Conklin, a Wilmurt native, when guiding a fishing party at the West Canada Lakes, was on the east side of South Lake and needed a boat so they started looking for one of Louie's.

"We looked around," Roc said, "and I was crossin' a log over a little ravine an' I spit, yo' know how a fellow'd do, an' I looked down, yo' know, to see where the spit was landin' an' I see a funny color down there, a little patch of strange green among th' leaves. I climbed down an' investigated an' there was one of Louie's boats asettin' in a little gully like an' covered with leaves. It was about fourteen feet long an' with it was oars an' paddle, a yoke, an ax an' a floatin' jack. We got th' boat out an' used it an' hid it again when we was through with it, all except that Furgusen Jack. It took my eye, an' I says to myself I said that'll come in handy. It come in handy all right. Beside usin' it for jackin' I used it right along for a buggy light."

Roc and his party went over to Louie's camp and found it locked. That didn't set so good with Roc, finding a lock on a camp so far back in the woods; but they managed to get in through one of the windows. They used Louie's stove and had a good feed. Hidden in the corner of Louie's woodshed they found a barrel of salt bearmeat with fat on it two inches thick, and

96

HARD AS LAURENTIAN GRANITE AND
TOUGH AS ADIRONDACK SPRUCE

THERE WAS SOMETHING ABOUT
LOUIE ONE HAD TO LIKE

TRUME HASKELL   "PONY" HASKELL

THE OLD FRANCIS WILKINSON PLACE
IN THE WOODS ABOVE NOBLEBORO

JOHN EDWARD SPENCER WILKINSON (UNCLE ED)

UNCLE ED'S WILMURT HOUSE

CAMP AT COW VLIE ON JOCKS LAKE ROAD

"PONY" HASKELL TAKES A PARTY
IN TO BARBER'S ON JOCKS LAKE

EAST END OF INDIAN CLEARING

JOCKS LAKE

"BY" CONGDON RAN THE LIVERY AT PROSPECT

HOTEL AT PROSPECT

HOTEL AT NOBLEBORO

AT MOREHOUSEVILLE
KREUZER'S HOTEL

BECRAFT'S PLACE
later Matteson's Mountain Home

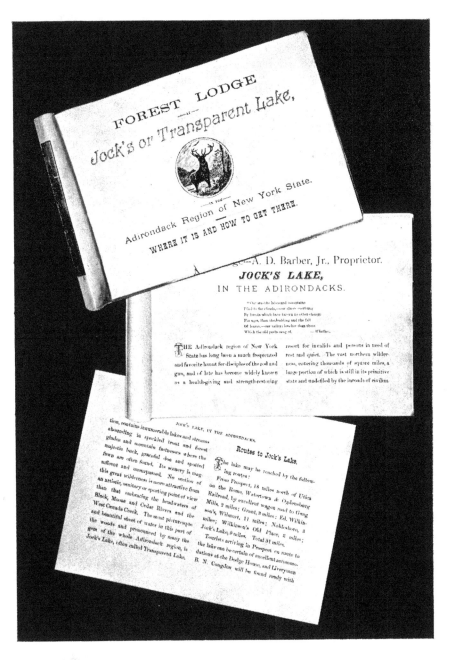

FOREST LODGE

Jock's or Transparent Lake,

IN THE

Adirondack Region of New York State.

WHERE IT IS AND HOW TO GET THERE.

A. D. Barber, Jr., Proprietor.

JOCK'S LAKE,

IN THE ADIRONDACKS.

> "Our sea-like lakes and mountains
> Piled to the clouds,—our rivers overflowing
> By forests which have known no other change
> For ages, than the budding and the fall
> Of leaves,—our valleys lovelier than those
> Which the old poets sang of." —*Whittier.*

THE Adirondack region of New York State has long been a much frequented and favorite haunt for disciples of the rod and gun, and of late has become widely known as a healthgiving and strength-restoring resort for invalids and persons in need of rest and quiet. The vast northern wilderness, covering thousands of square miles, a large portion of which is still in its primitive state and undefiled by the inroads of civiliza-

tion, contains innumerable lakes and streams abounding in speckled trout and forest glades and mountain fastnesses where the majestic buck, graceful doe and spotted fawn are often found. Its scenery is magnificent and unsurpassed. No section of this great wilderness is more attractive from an artistic, sanitary or sporting point of view than that embracing the headwaters of Black, Moose and Cedar Rivers and the West Canada Creek. The most picturesque and beautiful sheet of water in this part of the woods and pronounced by many the gem of the whole Adirondack region, is Jock's Lake, often called Transparent Lake,

Routes to Jock's Lake.

THE lake may be reached by the following routes:

From Prospect, 18 miles north of Utica on the Rome, Watertown & Ogdensburg Railroad, by excellent wagon road to Gang Mills, 2 miles; Grant, 3 miles; Ed. Wilkinson's, Wilmart, 11 miles; Nobleboro, 3 miles; Wilkinson's Old Place, 5 miles; Jock's Lake, 9 miles. Total 31 miles.

Tourists arriving in Prospect en route to the lake can be certain of excellent accommodations at the Dodge House, and Liveryman B. N. Congdon will be found ready with

FOREST LODGE

GROUP AT BARBER'S
Mrs. Barber on the porch. Left to right—
Andy Carmen, Frank Baker, the Carmen
sisters, Eddie Robertson, Giles Becraft,
and A. Dutton Barber himself

TROUT AND VENISON
OVERLAP AT BARBER'S

BARBER AND HIS CREW
John Hines. Nat Shepard. Frank Douglas. Ed Robert-
son, Fred Kreuzer. William Wilbur. Chas. Shepard,
Merrill Sprague. Frank Grove. A. D. Barber. Mary
Carmen, Ella Carmen, Molly Clancy, Kate Saltz-
man

Courtesy of Henry Hart

"Dut"

The Dog House
It was said that Barber had the best pack of
deer hounds in the whole North Woods.

BAKER WAS ALWAYS PLAYING
WITH THE BEAR AT BARBER'S

A PARTY OF YALE BOYS
Giles Becraft and Eddie Robertson, Guides

GILES BECRAFT AT OUTLET BROOK CAMP
LOOKING FOR A LOST DOG

GUIDE, FRANK BAKER

A PARTY FROM BARBER'S
On their way to the West Canada country
and Louie's.   Eddie Robertson, guide.

Photo by A. B. Gardner

packed down in the ice-hole there was a chunk of venison and some nice "salmon." When Louie returned to his camp the two silver dollars that he found on his kitchen table didn't make him feel any better about it. He couldn't spend them at the West Canada Lakes.

Roc Conklin was a great story teller and it was a real show to listen and watch him as he acted out what took place one day over in the Woodhull Lake country. A souvenir card had been published showing Roc posing with only four dead bear but each time Roc told the tale he added a bear or two. Here is a true account of what actually happened, as Roc told E. A. Spears, Utica newspaper man.

It was in the hunting season and Roc had a repeater slung over his arm. Five cartridges were in the gun. Five more were in his pocket.

All at once Roc became conscious of the presence of something mysterious and mighty. Some great power was about. He had walked right into the midst of an all-powerful atmosphere. What the —l was it?

Roc looked up. Two big bears not five rods away were moving toward him. They hadn't seen him. Their heads were swaying from side to side and their sharp-pointed gray noses twitched as they sniffed the air. They too seemed to sense that something was wrong.

In no time at all Roc fetched his rifle to his shoulder and planted a bullet between the eyes of each animal and did it so fast that both dropped at once.

Bears! Bears! Bears!

Then one of the most amazing things that ever happened took place. The whole woods blossomed with black bears. They sprang up everywhere. They shot out from the sides of trees. They loomed up from behind old stumps and fallen logs. For just a moment they stood all over the place, some on their hind legs, others on their haunches, or all fours. Everywhere a bear was taking one quick look. It was a vast still picture of bears.

They were looking at the surprised Roc Conklin, for the moment dumbfounded into inactivity.

"I must have walked right into a bear convention," said Roc.

Then the bears began to move. They ran every which way, some taking to trees.

As cool as an icicle Roc picked out the biggest of the lot that were running away and dropped them, one, two, three. That emptied his gun. Five bears were laid low. Others were fast getting out of sight and "a whole flock of them were climbing trees." That was a happy situation for Roc.

In no time at all he had his remaining five shells in his gun and "Then I went squirrel hunting for bears. I walked around to see which were the biggest ones, for having only five shells I couldn't get them all. After I looked them all over I dropped five out of the tree tops and you ought to see what a thump they made when one hit the ground.

"Well, there were 10 bears and no more cartridges and the tree tops were still full of them. I ran over to camp and got more ammunition but when I got back all the rest of the bears were gone, including the cubs and yearlings.

"Now, if I'd had my box of ammunition along I might just as well have got a real mess of bears."

Louie minded his own business and wanted others to mind theirs. After he had been staying alone and had not seen anyone for a long time, he was glad to see one come in. At such a time he would talk freely at first, thankful for companionship, and then suddenly, his social feeling satisfied, his uneasiness showed plainly that he wanted to be left alone. One could then take a walk and upon returning, if you paid little attention to him, you got along with him all right. When Louie did not like anyone, he wouldn't even give him a piece of string, he would not even look at him, and money did not mean a thing in gaining Louie's respect and friendship. He did not like those young tenderfoot sports who were always asking questions. He did

98

like children and liked to talk to them of woodcraft and the ways of animals.

When one person was in camp with him, Louie perhaps would talk, but when two or more were present, he would usually go quietly about his business. No matter how many were there, and even if there were only one besides himself, Louie almost always ate alone. Others got their own meals and ate in the larger room while he would brew his black tea, "so strong it float an iron wedge," cut up a few potatoes and fry them in his bear-lard, some meat if he had it, which he usually did, and sit on his bunk in his kitchen and eat the solitary meal. The kitchen was his private domain, for the sports never sat around it and Louie did not often go into the big room when they were gathered there.

Trume Haskell came to Louie's in all seasons and Louie liked him. They ate their meals together. After a day or so near camp Trume and Louie often packed what they needed, took their guns so as to have a little fresh meat, and went off into the woods. Many of these trips were to the Indian River country. The deeper wildness of those black stillwaters appealed to both of them. First comes Northrup Stillwater, then Louie, then Green Stillwater, the third one down. Green is so named because of the thick green timber, dark spruce and balsam, that crowds close on each side hanging low over the black water. Louie Stillwater was named after Louie himself.

On one trip they poked their heads through an opening in the evergreens on Green Stillwater, pulled aside the heavy branches and looked out and up and down the stream.

"We ought to have some fish," Trume said.

"Yo' tink da sam ting ah do me. Ah feesh, yo' get da meat."

A short distance farther on Louie went into the thick underbrush and brought out a little boat. As soon as he had pushed off into the stream, Trume started hunting up toward the ridge. The going was rough, over projecting shelves of rock and through deep cuts between them. At one place Trume climbed slowly up onto one of these ledges and looked over and down into the deep shadows of the pocket on the other side. A light colored surface caught his eye. There, built up to a big overhanging rock, he saw the roof of a camp shingled with shakes. He could hardly believe it. Then he saw the camp itself, made of perfect logs, well axed, a camp that would take two men a week or ten days to build. A wonderful camp for such a place.

He settled down with his rifle across his knees and took in every detail. One thing that attracted his attention was a great pile of deer hides, hundreds of them, piled at one side of the camp. Trume worked his way down, and as he came closer he was surprised at the completeness of it. The open end was close to the face of the rock against which the fires were built. It was fitted out with pots and pans, a woodsmade chair and table, everything that would be needed. There was no stove. Outside was a pile of two or three cords of fine split wood and the deer hides. Hides were then bringing about seventy-five cents each in Gloversville.

Trume returned to the stillwater following a narrow gully from the camp to the stream. Louie was just paddling in. He had a nice mess of trout.

"There's a camp back in here, Louie. Right back of those rocks."

"Ba da holy feesh! Wat for ol' Louie been long tam on dees wood! W'ere ees dat camp on?"

Louie followed Trume until they came to the camp. He appeared to be much surprised as he examined every little thing. They stayed there and later, when they were eating their trout, Louie looked at Trume and said slowly, "Ah t'ink, Trume, ba cripe, if dere's wan ting on dees wood ba gosh you find heem."

Trume smiled and said to himself, "The old boy knew it was here all the time."

"Yo' kip dees on your head," Louie said next morning as they were leaving.

Trume also came in to Louie's in the winter on snowshoes.

After staying a few days he asked where would be a good place to fish; he wanted some to take out.

"Wan place same lak oder," Louie told him as he rubbed his square chopped-off winter whiskers.

With a pack and some venison for bait, an ax and a dipper, Trume went over to Brook Trout Lake to chop a few holes in the ice, which he expected to find about two feet thick. He walked around the lake to the bay to the right of the outlet where he noticed some little heaps of snow and soon found three old holes. He opened one, got the snow out and baited up with a little spring pole. He cleaned out the other holes and set his lines. The water was very shallow, not over two or three feet deep, and there was a mud bottom. In a short time he caught thirty-five or forty pounds, which for Brook Trout Lake meant thirty-five or forty trout. They were pink bellied and exceptionally well colored.

When Trume came back Louie was in his kitchen. As soon as he saw the fish he said, "Ba gosh, yo' see ma sign."

They got along all right together but Trume had to be careful. Louie kept the main room neat and clean, even the glasses shone, although the place sometimes had a rotten smell because dozens of deerskins often would be hanging upstairs or a piece of meat somewhere getting ripe for trap bait. His kitchen, where he lived, was what Trume thought "a dirty hole." Trume made the mistake of offering to clean it up for Louie.

"If yo' don' lak it, Trume, maybe it was bettaire yo' don' stay," Louie told him.

Louie's outer clothing was usually pretty dirty. He changed his underwear now and then but no one ever knew him to take a bath except when he fell in, although he was a great man to wash his feet, washing them two or three times a week. It was his feet that took him through the woods.

At the beginning of one hunting season, Trume dropped his pack at Louie's door. Louie was not at home and Trume sat down to rest. It was one of those early fall days when the snakes come out of the shadows and coil up in the open places in the sun. In front of him, on a pile of deer bones, Trume saw a large snake, and then on the packed dirt another and still more. At least a half dozen snakes were within a few feet of him. He picked up a strong stick.

"Look at 'em. Right at the door of the camp," Trume thought as he went after them.

About an hour later Louie came and Trume was quick to tell him what he had done. "I killed four of them," he said. "Two got away."

Ye wolves and catamounts! Louie was the maddest Frenchman Trume had ever seen. "Boy, he'll never forgive me," ran through his mind. "That's the last of me and Louie."

Louie went inside of the camp, followed by Trume. They did not look at each other nor say a word as they started getting supper. Louie kept grunting to himself. As they ate, the air began to clear and Louie told Trume how he had carried those snakes all the way from Moose River and had put them in his garden to kill the potato bugs.

Before they went to bed Louie said, "Wan ting nevaire do. Nevaire keel no more snake."

Trume expected that he and Louie might take another little trip somewhere but early the next morning, before daylight, Louie got up quietly and went outside. Trume heard him walking away from the camp and heard him push the boat off through the thin shore ice and row away.

Trume ate his breakfast, took his pack and gun and somewhat aimlessly worked over south of Brook Trout Lake and north of the Indian River. He was mogging around on the Muskrat Creek near Indian Lake when he shot and wounded a big buck with the finest head that he had ever seen, a set of horns that he would never forget. He shot it on the edge of a swamp and tried for two days to get the wounded deer, but finally had to come away without it. He went back home by way of Cobblestone Brook, Jones Lake and the West Creek.

Early that winter he was again at Louie's place and he saw in the woodshed a deer's head which he recognized at once. He knew those horns. He had never seen anything like them for shape and size.

Trume told Louie the whole story of how he had wounded a buck in a swamp on the Muskrat with a head just like the one he had in the woodshed and had tried for two days to find it before giving up. Louie followed him closely. It all matched up.

Louie said he had found the deer about a half-mile in the swamp, just where Trume had told of wounding it Louie was trapping when he found it and fishers were working on it. It was the best find he ever made, for he caught five fisher on the carcass. Five!

He gave Trume the horns, who brought them out and had them set up. They had seventeen points, three crotches and a split crotch.

When the air was just right, from far to the west as from distant rumbling of thunderheads, Louie, from his northern camps, could hear the heavy blasting on the building of Webb's railroad where it was pushing its way north to join the New York

103

and Ottawa road at Tupper Lake. Wide, wild valleys and purple mountain ranges lay between but did not shut out that ominous sound. And to the east, lumbering was steadily approaching the Cedars up the Cedar River and those beautiful lakes could escape for but a year or two the destructive hand of the lumberman.

The Moose River Tract, for the most part, belonged to the Anson Blake estate, but during the past few years the greater portion of it had been bought up by the newly proposed club, The Adirondack League Club, for the avowed purpose of converting it into a park. The remaining lands, and South, Mud and Big West and the upper parts of the West Creek were the property of A. C. Hall, lumberman, who likewise announced his intention of establishing a park.

While there might have been some truths in the statements made by the parties controlling these lands that their chief object was the founding of parks, the guides and sportsmen familiar with the country knew different. The Moose River Tract was especially rich in spruce timber. With the water supply at their command the owners could float it to market at small expense.

Also the Indian, Johnny Leaf, who had been working for the tanneries around Newton Corners, had the nerve to build a bark shanty at the outlet of Mud Lake, which was not over a half mile from Louie's camp. Out at the Corners it was known that he would kill a deer for a pint of whiskey. He was a killer and Louie did not like to have him so near. Too near! It spoiled the country.

Were the days of the wilderness numbered, even at the West Canadas?

The League

Chapter Nine

In 1891 the Adirondack League Club was formed. It was a fish and game preserve of 120,000 acres, the largest sporting club of its kind in the world. In addition to the Blake Estate Tract of 85,000 acres, it secured control of Township No. Five containing 35,000 acres, which adjoined the Blake Tract. There were three lodges—the Bisby Lodge with its cottage colony and old fashioned comfort, the well patronized Mountain Lodge on Little Moose Lake near Old Forge, and Barber's Forest Lodge on Jocks Lake. The Jocks Lake camp was the first rendez-vous of the Club, the name of the Lake and Camp was changed to Honnedaga. A post office was established with Dut Barber as postmaster.

He also was appointed steward of the club and he ran the club house very much as he had run his own. Everything was rosy. The guides were quitting their old favorite tobacco, the woodsman's choice, the strong and fragrant "Warnicky Brown;"

actually giving up their "Warnicky"—temporarily—and smoking "Fruits and Flowers" and ten and fifteen cent cigars. Barber did not smoke much but would chew up a dozen or more "Roscoe Conklings" in a day. New buildings were erected and elaborate members cottages were built on the lake.

In addition to the state laws the members were governed by rules of the club. These forbade the taking of more than fifteen pounds of speckled trout or ten in number and the same limitation was put on fish carried from the preserve. Also, "jacking or floating for deer is absolutely forbidden." The members were convinced that jack hunting resulted in the wounding and maiming of more deer than were killed.

When the League took over Barber's, Webb's new Adirondack railroad made a station stop named Honnedaga between Remsen and Forestport Station and League members were informed that the new railroad ran within eight or nine miles of the lake and that a "carriage" road had been cut through to the head. This was good news for those who had traveled the torturous Jocks Lake road in from the Wilkinson Place near Nobleboro.

Mr. Edward Farrell wrote in the magazine, *Forest Leaves*, a quarterly published by the Sanitarium Gabriels at Gabriels, N. Y. which always carried on its first page, the line, "Come With Me Into the Wilderness and Rest." "There was no station building at Honnedaga so our trunks were dropped into the ditch and with the aid of the trainmen we climbed down to safety. A substantial farmhouse was within two hundred feet of the road and there we found excellent accommodations with farmer, Bion Kent. After carrying our trunks indoors we retired to sleep away the fatigues of a strenuous day.

"The next morning was radiant with early sunshine as Mr. Kent made himself ready for the trip to the lake and soon we were on our way. The air was full of the fragrance of the young balsams that had been slashed to let the sun's rays strike the road and when near the clearings, the notes of the songbirds were heard on every side. But the topsoil of the woods made a poor road covering and a heavy recent rain had flooded the low places and turned every boghole into a slough. The horses sank to their knees in the mud, the wheels were buried to the hubs, and we spent the next two hours climbing one side of the boulders only to splash down into deeper mud on the other.

"At last we reached a lake used as a reservoir for the Black River Canal. Here we stopped for rest and refreshments. We ate, rejoicing that we were able to open our mouths without having them filled with mud. After resting the horses two hours we started on the last three miles of the journey. The driver urged on his horses. While they moved out of a mud hole, our front wheels were poised on the brink ready to drop into it, and we clung to the seats in momentary danger of being dashed against the rocks or stumps. Thus we went forward at the rate of a mile an hour wondering if we would ever reach the lake. The silence of desperation closed around the party and I hated myself for selecting such a road. At last we arrived at the end of our ride and the horses hung their heads and panted and we let go our desperate grips on the seat-guards and heaved great sighs of relief.

"Cheerfulness succeeded hours of gloom, and we were soon seated in a guide boat with our trunks safely placed in another and a moment later the lake in all its loveliness was spread out before us. The sun was declining in the west. The sky was cloudless and the atmosphere was filled with an amber light that increased the beauty of the spruce-clad shores. The sweet west wind was not strong enough to ruffle the surface of the lake, so we floated onward over a burnished sheet of water. The guides replied to inquiries but the conversation was desultory. The all-pervading beauty of the scene prevented remarks upon special features of the landscape. As we approached the club-house, the sun dropped below the hills.

"A few minutes later we were welcomed to the clubhouse as guests of one of the members. The supper was soon served and the party of ten or twelve joined in animated conversation, the old road and the new being the principal topics.

"Our month's visit came to an end all too soon. We were

determined to leave by the old road, by way of Nobleboro, in order to make a visit to Morehouseville, and arrangements had been made for us to go out that way.

"Soon after breakfast we heard the blasts of the horn, warning us that the livery had arrived at the landing on the opposite shore. We crossed the lake accompanied by all the guests, seated ourselves in the buckboard and bid goodbye to the pleasantest party we ever met in the woods. My pipe was ready for lighting the minute we started, but at the end of the first rod we mounted a boulder. I was obliged to drop the match and clutch the guard rails. For the next hour we clung to the seats, rolling and pitching. Streams of perspiration ran down our faces. I dared not let go long enough to take the pipe out of my mouth. The sand worked in between our fingers and wore the skin from our hands while we went forward at angles that threatened to throw us over the horses or drop us one side into the morass. Fortunately the horses and driver knew the road. They drew the wagon over the logs and stones and dropped it into the gulf beyond, then, pausing a moment, surmounted the next obstruction and dragged us after them. At length we rested to breathe the horses. A member of the club who was on the way out said that they had left the road in bad condition to discourage visits from stray fishermen. The plan may have proved successful. It certainly subjected travelers to hours of misery. Our troubles ended when we reached Haskell's, Wilkinson's old place. The old road is worse than the new."

Another party had something to write home about. The letter read: "Our first camping trip took us to the long stillwater on the West Canada Creek. We had an ample pack-basket of provisions, a generous supply of blankets and other luxuries, a light but substantial boat and two good guides to manage the outfit. The trail led through the forest and was easily traveled in two hours. While one guide made camp, our other guide, Giles Becraft, took us fishing. A logging dam at the foot of the stillwater had changed it into a long narrow lake. Trees were growing out of the shallows along the margin and their branches formed arches high above the stream. The air was still, except

108

when the kingfishers rattled out their shrill notes or the old ducks warned their broods. Giles knew where to go and he had real success with the trout so that when we returned to our camp our table was well supplied. Darkness set in before we were ready to eat. One side of the log hut consisted of an immense boulder and the fire burned brightly against it. The balsam bed was opposite, with a space of two or three feet between. We sat along the foot of the bed. The trout were broiled by means of crotched sticks over a bed of coals and a lump of butter was dropped into each fish as it was served. Appetite, good digestion and health assisting both made our wildwood meal a memorable feast."

All of Barber's guides stayed on with the League and new men came, good guides like Jim Wadsworth, Jim Putney, Fay Brown, Bert Lindsay, Nat Shepard and Jim Dalton. The guides were paid thirty-five dollars a month and they picked up about thirty-five more.

Frank Baker, who had been head guide for Barber, was still considered the foremost guide in that section of the woods. He not only knew how to get to where he was going, but he was handy, and if something happened to a boat or a yoke he knew how to fix it. In fact, any guide had to be a sort of handy man, sometimes even a carpenter or a plumber. Baker knew that he was good and it went against his grain to have anyone catch a bigger trout or shoot a bigger buck than he. Louie didn't get along very well with Baker. For one thing Baker hated snakes, was deathly afraid of them, and whenever he was at Louie's he did not hesitate to let him know it. To Louie, Baker was the kind that would eat and drink everything in sight, but when it came to washing dishes or getting a pail of water would expect others to do it.

Baker showed his temper once when in camp on Little Indian Lake. He was flipping flapjacks and missed one, half of it landing on top of the stove. He promptly kicked the sheet iron stove right out from under the stove-pipe and nearly set the camp afire. He evidently wasn't as good at the flipping art as John Heirs. At his camp between Big Rock and Metcalf Lakes, with its inside fireplace, old John would flip a cake so that anyone on the outside of the camp could see it come up out of the top of the chimney, take a turn or two in the air, and drop back down into the chimney again. John, inside, would catch it neatly in the frying pan. That's right.

But Baker had a head on his shoulders and a good system for using it. He not only knew the woods but knew how to cook. To many hungry fishermen Baker's deep blueberry pies, baked in a reflector oven before the open fire, were a great treat never expected in the backwoods. And he was clean and his meals were appetizing and tasty.

Baker's life had always been close to the woods. When still a boy on the farm, he didn't mix with the others and younger boys in the neighborhood spoke of Frank Baker as one might have spoken of Daniel Boone. It was something for the young kids to even see him. They looked at him with awe. He was a great hunter who went off into the big woods all by himself.

There was one happening that didn't put any feathers in Baker's hat. A man named Michaels went back off the road a piece at Green Clearing to pick up a few apples from beneath a tree. He was filling his pockets when a set gun exploded and sent a charge of buckshot into his leg above his knee. He managed to get to Nobleboro where Doctor Morey of Grant was called. The leg was amputated and he lived for seventeen days. Perhaps if he had been killed instantly someone might have been held to blame. As it was nothing was done; it was just an accident. But little groups of men, speaking softly, seemed to know that it was Frank Baker who had set that gun under the apple tree for bear.

Another outstanding guide, who had been with Barber and who stayed on with the League, was Giles Becraft. His home was on a small clearing on the edge of a beautiful stillwater on the East Branch of the West Canada Creek, where his father had settled around 1850 and ran "Becraft's Place" which later became Matteson's Mountain Home. Back of the house to the north were the mountains, rising two thousand feet in two

110

miles, covered with dense forest, and to the South was More-houseville and more clearings on the main road and beyond them the wilderness again. And here Giles had grown up from a boy and knew the country intimately for miles around, an "expert with a gun and a master hand at tempting the most cautious trout to take the fly." Those at Barber's or the League who had Giles Becraft for their guide had the best of companions as well as a man who knew the woods thoroughly.

The founding of the League was a sign that the Adirondacks were becoming more popular. All over the woods guides were more in demand; and the first annual meeting of the Guides Association was held at Saranac Lake in March, 1892, with more than two hundred attending. As each succeeding spring brought more fishermen into the wilderness, as each fall brought more hunters, more of the League members made the trip to Louie's place. The years were passing but he felt as young as ever. He had pride in being the owner of a place that attracted the honest and unpretentious people. It was character and decency that Louie recognized and respected, and he could quickly distinguish that from any affectation based on money alone. The sports stayed at his camps and used his boats. Important in their own world on the outside, they made themselves at home, did their own cooking and dishwashing and ate much from Louie's garden and had Louie's maple syrup on their pancakes. They paid him well for the use of his camp, the use of wood and kerosene and tallow candles, and for the use of his boats. Besides money they gave him fish rods, guns, knives and various little presents. At one time he had four rifles and a shot gun. He had a 44 Winchester, a 38-40, a 30-30 and a 38-55. He used the 38-40 '73 model mostly, the caliber that had been used by Buffalo Bill and American pioneers in the west. He carried a large half hunter silver watch and a compass that someone had given him. He enjoyed having the right kind of men near him, and he would often say and mean it, "You owe me noting. Ah have good tam, sam lak you." However, he did not tell them of his best fishing places, especially the summer spring holes which he always kept secret. Once on the Indian he met a warden from the League. Louie had a wonderful mess of trout but when asked where he had caught them, lest he had caught them on League property, he said, "Oh, ah git dem. Ah got a place."

Among the doctors, lawyers, manufacturers, business men, politicians who frequented the club, there came two ministers who were such enthusiastic swimmers that they would rather swim than fish. Two or three times a day they plunged in at Louie's split rock boat landing. He watched them. In all his wanderings he had never learned to swim.

"Anybody can swim," they told him. "Look at the animals. They all swim. All you have to do, Louie, is jump in. Like this."

A day or two after they went out Louie walked down to the boat landing. It was toward evening and the lake was as still as glass, the water transparent to the bottom through the six or eight foot depth right off the rock. "Anybody can swim," Louie pondered, "all you have to do is jump in. Look at the animals. They all swim." He pulled off his clothes. There was no one to see him but swallows dipping low over the water, a hawk circling high in the sky, a few gulls, and no doubt many sharp little beady eyes looking out from the leafy shoreline. Louie stood there on the rock, his body so unnaturally white. Then he jumped. The hawk screamed. The gulls rose and flew off toward Brook Trout. A squirrel chattered. And he went straight to the bottom.   .

His finger tips were torn and bleeding and his nails broken by his climb up the side of the rock to the surface. Sometimes, later on, when the water was quiet and with no ripple, he would point down to two indentations in the rock, which he said had been made by his heels when he struck bottom. What puzzled him though, the one thing he said he could never figure out, was why two ministers would lie to him like that and nearly drown him.

One afternoon Louie watched a boat as it came out from the Twin Lakes trail and headed straight across to the camp. A League Club guide and a boy in the boat pulled alongside at Louie's landing.

"We got two bear cubs up a tree, Louie. Mike Lyons is watching them. Will you go back with us and help us catch them?"

Louie had no relish for Mike. Mike had too foul a mouth.

"W'ere be they?"

"Near the trail. Not so far."

"W'at you want ees blanket, box, nails. You got ax? Take dees wan."

Louie went into the camp and put two blankets in his pack basket. In the shed out back he found a box which he handed to the boy. "We were roaming around over here in your territory, Louie, just for the fun of it," the guide said as the boy rowed the boat, "and we ran into a bear and a couple of cubs. The old one ran off as fast as she could go but the two cubs went whining up a young maple. Mike, he's set on gettin' the cubs alive. 'Go get Louie', he said. Mike was tying the boy's red sweater around the tree when we left him."

Near the top of the rise of ground on the trail they hollered and heard Mike answering them. They went through the woods to where he was waiting for them with the cubs.

Louie handed one of the blankets to Mike. "Ah chop de tree," Louie told him. "You jomp queek on heem wid de blanket."

"Sure, Louie, I know," Mike said.

"Dose cub, he don't be slow."

The tree was chopped down and there was an awful scramble as they jumped on the cubs with the blankets the instant that they touched the ground. A little rap on the snoot quieted them.

As they were being put in the box Mike was polluting the clean mountain air with a blue streak of blasphemy. Louie hesitated. One certain move of the slat in Louie's hand and a cub would be disappearing into the brush, and a ten dollar bounty too, if that's what Mike was looking for. There was a bounty on bear for a few years around 1892. Louie looked at Mike and waited and Mike understood.

"Dat's bettaire," Louie told Mike. "Dees cub, he ees too

young." Louie tried the slats. "Some day he grow oup. jus sam lak dat wan on Jocks."

Louie returned to camp. The others stayed that night on Brook Trout and the next day they went with the bear cubs along the Indian to the club house on Bisby Lake.

The frightful condition of the roads into Honnedaga Forest Lodge caused the patronage to fall off. Bisby and Little Moose lodges were being favored. To correct things, the club's own "Snyder Boulevard" was built between Honnedaga and South Lake. Roads were also put through from White Lake to Wood-hull and from Sand Lake to North Lake. A $30,000 appropriation was expected to improve the old road to Buffalo Head and much work was put on the five-mile stretch between Reed's and North Lake. Of this a club report said, "Over the last mile, on the North Lake end, which once took an hour, members of the board drove last November in six minutes."

But all the road work did not come up to expectations and the following year "about half of the nineteen-mile ride to Honnedaga was delightful, a quarter of it was endurable and the rest was misery." And the club at Honnedaga was slipping. To bolster it up they let Barber go and Bion H. Kent was engaged as new manager. Dut Barber was all through. The spring had run dry. The New York poker players had been too smart for him. It was quite a comedown for Dut when he went to working on the road for the town for he was soft, too soft. He who had been the great host had lost everything, lost his own money, lost his wife's money, and because his money was gone he seemed to have lost his friends and men's confidence. When he left that neck of the woods Byron Cool said he owed him three dollars and a half for a laundry bill.

White Tiger and Beans

Chapter Ten

And then came the lumbering.

In the fall of '91 they built the lumberdam at the outlet of Mud Lake.

It was a bitter pill to take for the fishermen and hunters of the West Canada country. One of the first parties of "outsiders" to come in after the dam had been built was a party from Albany. After a day's ride on train and stage they arrived at Newton Corners about sundown on the seventh of May 1892. Here they were met by Jim Sturges who informed them that everything was in readiness for the fishing. Louie had come out from the West Canadas that morning and told them that. with the exception of a few cakes floating around, the ice was out of the lakes. After a comfortable night at Dave Sturges' they started in with Louie and Jim, passing the Sacandaga fish hatchery, the last habitation, two miles from the Corners, and arriving at Pillsbury Lake, twelve miles distant, that afternoon.

Considerable snow and ice were encountered along the trail, especially while ascending the Blue Ridge. They crossed the inlet of the lake on the ice in order to get at the boats. After a night at Louie's Pillsbury camp they continued their tramp next day under heavy packs to the West Canadas.

No change in the trails from former years was noted until they neared Whitney Stream, the outlet of Pillsbury and Whitney Lakes. Whereas previously it had been customary to cross this brook and follow a trail to Mud Stream, half a mile beyond, and ascend this to Mud Lake, they now turned abruptly to the left and made their way a quarter of a mile along the bank of Whitney Stream where they took to the boats and rowed down into Mud Lake.

The stream was far above its natural level, the alders nearly submerged and the water extending several feet up the tree trunks on the banks. Mud Lake, heretofore a shallow pond where a dozen or more deer might have been seen feeding, presented a like appearance.

After crossing the lake they rowed up the outlet of Big West instead of going on the old trail, and carried around the little falls and over the short second carry, saving in this way a tramp of a half mile. South Lake was also flooded several feet.

This party stayed at Louie's for two weeks. The fishing they found poorer than ever before. Although they had no difficulty in obtaining an abundance of fish, they were small in comparison with those of other years. Owing to the cold weather the suckers had not come into the inlets so they were obliged to use minnows trolling. They caught no lake trout exceeding five and one-half pounds and the brook trout averaged but one-half pound. Two men from Gloversville, Burr and Steele, came in on the fifteenth. They caught on a spoon a brook trout which weighed two pounds and fourteen ounces and measured twenty inches.

Fly fishing was good when the weather permitted. Snow fell for three days. The ground and the mountains were covered and bore a real wintry look.

On two weeks' fishing trips of other years it was no unusual thing to see from fifty to one hundred deer during the stay but on this trip they saw but two, and those at Brook Trout Lake. Louie said that they had gone to the Cedars, Twins and the Moose River and that they would return as soon as the lumbermen let the water out of Mud Lake.

The lumbermen were now in the woods near the West Canadas. They were cutting on the West Creek six miles below the Mud Lake dam and it was expected that operations would be begun on South Lake before another year. All the agitation to make the Adirondack wilderness into a state park to save its virgin wildness seemed to have been lost.

Of the men who came into the woods for the lumberjobs there were many who could chop, build corduroy roads and handle teams but too few who could drive logs down the rivers. Many of the cant dogs but few peaveys. Real log drivers were wanted, all around lumberjacks, and the lumber companies brought men from the other side of the woods, from Maine, Canada and New Brunswick. They were good white-water men, hard drivers, hard workers and hard drinkers. Some brought their axes with them, guarding them closely. Most of these men had seen the northern and eastern Adirondacks first, the lower Racquette, the Saranac, the North River, the Schroon and the tough old Boreas. They had learned a few things on the North River— the upper Hudson—on that stretch at the Big Bend near the Deer Run and farther down where there was always a jam at Moulton Bars.

Sol Carnahan and his brothers Ab and Irv from New Brunswick were among the newcomers. On one Fourth of July a group gathered on the Black River bridge at Bellingertown near Forestport, facing upstream toward the white water. The stream was in flood. They waited expectantly. And then Sol came, riding a spruce log in the mad water. The crowd cheered and Sol held his peavy, not crossways like an ordinary log driver, but straight up before him, and sailed beneath them under the bridge. He was a riverman. In a holiday spirit he was just showing them how. Sol could ride a log in his rubber soled pacs.

117

"He could ride a bubble if he had to." He became a big jobber and was not one to show off when there was work to be done.

Jobber Jim McBeth was another one. His younger brother, Gene, drove river with Sol on the West Creek. Jim Hill was there too.

The Frenchmen would get Jim Hill's goat by forever telling about the big log jams in Canada. "Hold on, boys," Jim would say, "I remember I was in Canada once myself and I saw a big jam there too," and he would tell them the old story again about the biggest jam. "We had a hundred thousand pieces, got 'em sluiced out of the dam all right, all goin' down an' they was a pickin' up in the rear pretty fast. On the fourth day we rounded a big bend and by golly we met another drive comin' up. That was the biggest jam I ever saw."

Carnahan, Huckabone, Flansburg, Flanagan, McBeth, Conklin, Harvey, Whelan, Brown, Potter. "Get right in there. It won't burn yo'," they would holler and it wouldn't burn one either, for those driving floods were full of floating ice.

Among the first tote-teamsters on the West Creek were Will Hewitt and Tom Shaney, who toted in that first summer with oxen and wood-shod sleds from Big Brook. Horses were used the following winter on the ice-roads, and in the spring so much corduroy had been laid that oxen were not used any more, although sleds were still used on the roads farthest up. Horses could do the job. Each year they would go in a little farther with wheels, or with "scoot an' drag". The camps usually stocked up with all they needed before the breakup in the spring, for at that time, when the roads were at their worst with mud and high water, much of the stuff had to be carried in from the tote-teams to the driving camps in pack baskets. There were men, such as Big Joe Cote, who carried a pack basket all spring. He would much rather carry hundred pound packs than drive river.

Lumbering, at last, had really come to the big woods far up the old West Creek, and now Louie from his little canoe saw much change in his stillwaters high and wide from the new dams, and he heard the ring of the ax, the falling of the trees,

118

the voices of the lumberjacks, where before he had known only wild solitude.

Chevarie & Gendreau, jobbers, employing over two hundred men, had a camp on the Second Stillwater with an all French crew. They hauled their supplies on wood-shod sleds from the supply camp at Big Brook, following the old Hinckley & Ballou road north from the Jocks Lake road to the mouth of the Indian. From there on they cut a new road along the bank of the West Creek. Big Canadian bateaux, twenty-five feet long, with eight oars, were hauled in on the hard winter ice-road. One Frenchman plowed some beaver meadow land north of the Second Stillwater and raised potatoes for the camps and his place was called "The Farm."

These early jobbers soon learned that many of the methods that they had used in Canada did not work on the old West Creek. The mountains were rough and steep and rocky, and so were the streams. The long bateaux could not swing and dodge the big boulders. Log drivers who went up the creek with their chins up had their troubles. Chevarie & Gendreau had financial difficulties and that spring all men and horses dropped everything where they happened to be and walked out of the woods. Horses in the barns were headed out. Horses in the woods were unhooked, the sleighs left standing on the roads. They were driven out

119

to Wilmurt Corners where nearly a hundred horses were pastured after being turned over to the Hinckley Mercantile Company. The lumber company went back to Canada leaving its crews unpaid. The Trenton Falls Company, who had bought stumpage as far as Mud Lake, took over and carried on the work.

In the fall of 1890 Joe Mitchell of Indian Lake built a dam at the foot of the Second Stillwater, and Jobber Charley Swanson from Stony Creek had a camp at the foot of the First Stillwater and built a dam there. A large "headquarters camp" was established at "The Farm," from which supplies and equipment were distributed over the rough tote-roads to the camps about the woods.

When Charley Swanson was constructing the dam at the First Stillwater he dug up a human skull. Did this skull belong to one of the two Salisbury trappers who never came back and were they the two men whom it is believed that Morgan of Old Forge killed and robbed of their furs that winter around 1810?

The story goes that around that year a trapper from Moose River by the name of Morgan trapped with Green White as far east as the West Canada region. White was a decent sort of fellow but Morgan was not to be trusted, a murderer. One winter, when returning down the West Creek along by the Second Stillwater, they saw snowshoe tracks of two men who had crossed their line. Morgan swore that they were robbing traps. White's persuasion did no good so they separated as Morgan took after them. White returned to the Forge and told of the tracks and of Morgan following them. The next day Morgan came in. Chase, Wood, Williams and two other trappers were there and tried to find out something but Morgan considered it none of their business. Green White knew well enough what had happened when he saw Morgan's pack of furs double the size he had when they separated only the day before. The same season two trappers from Salisbury did not return from the trap lines and no sign was ever found of them. The old hills hold many secrets.

Among the lumberjacks, who was "the best man on the crick" was always open to argument. Tom McCauley's men would

120

never admit that any of Sol Carnahan's gang were better than they. But whatever gang he was in, a man had to make good in the woods or he would soon be shacking down the trail.

Most of them agreed that Pat Whelan was the best chopper. On the other side of the woods before crosscuts were used he had chopped seventy logs in a day, working just as fast toward night as he did in the morning. Those who saw him when he stepped up to a tree and planted his feet knew he was good. The way he could handle an ax was nothing short of marvelous. He used a three and a half pound ax with a quarter pound wedge in it. He was a big-framed raw-boned fellow who always played square, never looked for trouble and no one ever bothered him. He was not only the best chopper in the woods but was the best kicker in the bar-rooms outside. Pat's footprint could be seen on the ceilings all the way from Foote's place in Piseco to Murphy's Hotel in Prospect.

Rube Dunning was the best boatman. Fred Washburn run the boat with Rube. With an oarsman, bowsman and sternsman, they would drop down with the current above a jam that was forming. As they were passing it, the bowsman would catch a log in the jam with his pole and they would stay with it until it hauled; sometimes it would plug and stop again. If the boat was swept past the jam without the bowpole getting a hold, they would have to rope it up along the shore and try again. Rube would put a boat through water where no one else dared. In rough water they always pointed directly upstream.

Most any of them would have to admit that Ned Fournier was a champion log roller. He handled four hundred logs a day, piling them up on the skidway, rolling for a pair of horses where another man would have hard work rolling for one horse.

There were a lot of good toters. It is hard telling who was best, but there wasn't any argument when someone said that Johnny McCullen was good. He was a little fellow, short but strong and wiry; always laughing, always good natured, a hard drinker between trips but not on the road or on the job. Like any other good toter, he never hung on with his hands, just seemed to roll with each lurch of the wagon and never fall off. He liked horses and kept his tote teams fat. They would "shine like a bottle."

Ab Carnahan was "the best riverman that ever looked at the creek." Gene McBeth was good too.

No one wanted to dispute that big Joe Cote could carry the heaviest packs. And everyone knew that Tom Grimes was the funniest and Paul Hoppe was the "fightenest" man on the whole "crick." Then there was Johnny Leaf, the Indian, who "killed more deer than any other ten men in the woods."

Oh, there were all kinds of "best men on the crick." Indeed, they were all good. But with all the best men there was always some old fellow who had something to say about it. "When it come time to eat he didn't wait for no boatman to go and fetch 'im. He'd hop on a log an' ride across, balancing himself with his peavey or pike pole. When the jam broke he didn't run for no damn boat. Just jump on a log. I've seen 'im at Hess' Rifts. At Hess' Rifts too, mind yo'. Ask Rube."

Such men as Johnny McCullen, Mel Paul and Tom Burns, "could put a tote-team where some men could not even carry a halter." Johnny was a popular fellow and a good toter. On the road he hardly tightened a line, just geed and hawed, and like all who loved horses was always talking to them.

The teamster, leaving light, started out from the Mitchell or Second Stillwater with a team and jumper in the early morning. At Swanson's he changed to wheels and reached the headquarters camp at Nobleboro that night. The next day, with around fifteen hundred pounds, he started back, going as far as the mouth of the Indian. After putting up for the night he threw off half of his load and continued on to the Swanson or First Stillwater. The next morning he put half of his load on to a jumper and took it up to the Mitchell. From the Mercantile Company at Gang Mills, over the long flat stretches to Nobleboro, and on the doubling back, would take one toter about two weeks to get the full thirty hundred pounds to the headquarters camp on the Mitchell Stillwater.

They always carried extra shoes and if a horse sprung a

122

shoe they would stop and replace it using the same old holes in the hoof with the nails rasped off or nearly off, so a horse stepping on his shoe would pull off the shoe instead of breaking his foot.

There was one place in the woods where Johnny McCullen, distributing loads with his jumper, left one lumbercamp and hours later looked down on the same camp from high up on the mountainside. He had been traveling a switch-back sled-road up to the ridge where he could cross to a camp in the next valley. The tote-roads were not log-roads. Log-roads always ran from the high point down. Tote-roads had bad hills.

The teamsters often had a bunkhouse of their own, but among the lumberjacks it was common backwoods belief that the teamsters were not so exclusive as they thought they were, but had simply been segregated because of their strong, horsy smells and because they would be the first ones up in the morning disturbing the whole bunkhouse.

One of the biggest, if not the biggest, log-drives in the history of the whole North Woods went down the old West Creek in the spring of 1895. To be exact it was 20,194,156 feet board measure. It was nearly all spruce with just a few sticks of hemlock. All saw-logs, no pulp. They drove for sixty-nine days that year. That was the year of the big jam.

Louie, with his pack on his back, was going out of the woods at the time and from the tote-road alongside the creek he could see the lumberjacks working on the drive. He met them on the road. Many knew him.

"Hello, Louie. How's things up your way?" This from Pat Whelan, champion chopper who could make the chips fly as though it was snowing.

"She's good," Louie replied.

"Workin' for the company, Louie?" Pat asked.

"Ah work, me, on de road som tam dees wintaire. Bert Lebenwort camp. Moch bettaire for trap."

"Would be for you."

A great dynamite blast boomed and echoed from the direction of the river.

"Jam below Outlet Brook. She's keyed up so tight an' full o' bark an' stuff that the water can't get through."

Louie followed a side trail to one of the driving camps. He could hear the shouting of the men on the big creek. He saw them running and waving to one another.

"Get off."

"Get off."

"GET OFF."

The flood had hit the upper end of the jam. The men were scrambling to safety. Louie, from a rise of ground, could look upstream and see the lower half of the great mass of logs. A low muffled grinding ripping sound was heard and far up the creek Louie saw the water roar down over the top of the jam, piling the logs until they were twenty feet above the shore, but still the jam held solid. The men worked on it but accomplished nothing. Again the men saw the tail end raise, saw the rear end coming toward them, piling up. They ran, looking for a place to get off. The jam started to haul. One lumberjack, Trume Brown, after running some distance, found where he could jump into a big birch tree on the edge. He jumped, climbed up and out on a limb, and just as the jam uprooted the birch, he swung to the ground. Other men were hanging to trees as the jam went by, hoping their trees would hold. Other trees along the shore, some two feet through, were being mowed down or uprooted.

The water and logs and debris tore down over the jam. The whole jam was hauling now but when the water subsided the logs were plugged as bad as before. Louie went back to the driving camp and stayed there that night.

Just after breakfast, a little after five, Sol Carnahan, the jobber, stopped in the driving camp on his way up the creek.

"She's going to haul tomorrow morning," he told the men, "and I want every man of you off the river by ten o'clock. Bill Harvey's goin' to pull his sticks an' when his water hits the Swanson that'll be tripped. We'll trip both dams on the Indian. She's timed right and will hit around ten o'clock an' it's goin' to be one hell of a head o' water." Before he left them he warned them again, "Not a man on the logs after ten o'clock."

Early the next morning they were out picking at the logs. The forenoon went fast. The water was low and all was quiet and peaceful. There was no confusion. The face of the jam was as solid as a fort. Why hurry? There's more than an hour yet.

"What's that noise?"

"Wind. Sounds like wind blowing through the trees."

"Listen. My gosh, fellows, that ain't wind!"

"Water!"

"It can't be. We got an hour yet!"

"IT'S WATER! SHE'S HIT! GET OFF!"

It was upon them before they knew it. Sandy Flanagan just made the shore. Ab Carnahan and Dan Kennedy were on the same log as it swung out into the current below the jam.

"JUMP! GRAB A BUSH!" Ab cried, but Dan had already leaped. The water took him but he had hold of a branch and was

125

pulling himself to safety as the log with Ab on it shot away. Ab tried to ride it down, and for a moment it looked as though he might do the impossible. The mass of the jam was right behind him, plunging, tearing, grinding. The men on the shore watched him go. They saw the log throw Ab nearly ten feet into the air. One instant he was there and the next, nothing was to be seen but logs, end over end, standing upright, nosing under. The great turmoil of spruce logs swept over the place where Ab had disappeared. He never had a chance.

The men worked along the shore looking for some sign of Ab. Louie was there when they pried him loose from under a corner jam at the head of an island about a third of a mile below, a mutilated body with a broken neck.

For a while there was surly grumbling in the camps when the men learned that, down at the big boom before the flood they had sent their woods boss up the creek. He had gone by saddle horse to all the dams and had given his orders. The dams were opened one hour earlier than Sol had told them. The flood had hit the jam at nine o'clock instead of ten.

The water went low one spring and hung up the drive. Sol paid off his men and they headed out, most of them getting past the seven or eight bars north of the Flansburg Bridge and making it to Utica. But the next day it rained and kept on raining and the creek came up and Sol hustled to Utica to get his men. Starting on Main Street in Utica, near the depot, then along Whitesboro Street and across the river in Deerfield, he went from one bar to another rounding them up. He sent word to By Congdon at Prospect to have the teams and rigs ready at the station.

It wasn't the sluicing a dam before daylight, "sackin' the rear," or pig-yoking that they went back for, nor the beans, nor the chance of getting caught in the wood and getting drowned, nor standing around in a cold rain waiting for it to get light enough to go to work. And it wasn't the ninety cents, or a little better, a day, sixteen hours a day, seven days a week. It was something that's hard to explain. They had a job to do and it was their job as much as it was Sol's. They were proud, those jacks,

126

and that was the kind of men they were. "The wood's begun to move. The creek is up. Sol wants us back!"

When the train pulled into Prospect, By was there with his four-seaters and his long Welsh wagons to take them up the creek. It was now a driving flood, and most of the wood got down to the big boom.

The men sometimes drove the stillwaters at night, booming them in with a catspaw. If the wind was strong against them, blowing upstream, they might have to wait for two or three hours for it to change, if it changed at all. There was nothing to do then but idle around a big fire upon the shore. But if the wind did let up or change, the boss broke in on the circle with, "Come on Boys," and they moved quickly to the boats and to the windlass and got the old catspaw working. With a windlass anchored to trees, turned with a heavy iron winch or strong birch poles, they pulled the boom, pushing the logs ahead. No current, no windlass and boom could push the logs against a strong wind, and to work the windlass at such a time would break the boom. But the wind usually went down at night.

Louie stayed at the Seabury driving camp that night, and the following day he went his way down the tote-road toward Nobleboro, down the riverbank trail, over Big Brook bridge, through the balsam flat to where the tote-road joins the road to Jocks. A mile farther he came to the Haskell Place where he went inside to see Trume and heard about Bud Smith who had got caught in Haskells Rifts. Another good lumberjack gone. A man who could have sent his men into the danger spot but went himself instead.

From then on, for over a week, from Haskell's clear down to Bill Wright's and the Hubbard House, wolf howls and owl hoots and shouts of "Louie, da boy," let everyone know that French Louie was out of the woods.

And then one day Louie woke up and found himself lying in the grass back of Bill Wright's. He pulled himself together. He felt in his pockets. His money was gone. There was a commotion in the front yard and he walked to the corner of the building to see what was going on. Just off the porch the lumberjacks were having their fun. Three men stood on a whiskey keg and the first one to fall off had to pay for the drinks. Others were playing bear, driving a man around on his hands and knees with a pair of reins.

An old river-bull hollered, "Look at 'em. I run th' river in moccasins. Now they have to have calked boots an' hemlock wid th' bark on."

This was at Wright's, one of the places where the lumberjacks headed for when they left the camps and came down for their fun, where they gathered after log-rolling before the river driving began; when, uneasy like animals on a leash, they waited for the spring thaws, south winds and rains, and at Wright's bar plenty of them filled their hides with all they could put away after the drive was down.

Bill Wright had always lived in the Wilmurt section and he knew the ways of these men. As a boy, he worked for old Dick Paul, the famous bear hunter who had lived near the covered bridge at the falls. Young Bill had dragged a cod-fish on a rope through the woods for fifty cents a day and found. He would be gone all day up Black Creek and Black Creek Lake way and a bear would follow that scent for a week or two afterwards. There were big flocks of wild pigeons around Black Creek in those days. There was a pigeon roost where the trees were so covered with the birds

ATWELL MARTIN, THE HERMIT OF NORTH LAKE

Photo by Gardner & Frey

JOHNNY LEAF'S CAMP AT MUD LAKE DAM

FRESH MEAT HANGING FROM THE CROSS POLE

JOHNNY LEAF
Would kill a deer for a pint of whiskey

SETH LYON'S PLACE
Between Buffalo Head and North Lake

Ray Dunham at the well — Photo by the Author

NAT SHEPARD'S CABIN
ON SEABURY STILLWATER
Later Johnny Leaf's

AT THE HASKELL PLACE

ATWELL MARTIN'S WIGWAM
At North Lake. where
he lived for forty years

"DUT" BARBER'S FIRST CAMP

BUILDING THE DAM ON SEABURY STILLWATER

BERT LEAVENWORTH'S LUMBER CAMP
No sawed lumber was in this camp at Sampson Bog

SOL CARNAHAN

A GOOD LOAD

KREUZER'S MOREHOUSEVILLE LUMBERJACKS

HESS' RIFTS WERE ROUGH

COME AND GET IT!

THE KNIFE THAT LOUIE
CARRIED MANY YEARS
*Given to the Author by
Geo. Wilson of Indian Lake*

A NICE "SALMON"

TOM GRIMES

THE DRIVE HUNG UP

SACKING THE REAR

BATTEAU

SCOOT 'N DRAG

ON THE INDIAN RIVER

AN ADIRONDACK DUGOUT
The author
(*some time ago*)

ROC CONKLIN AND HIS BEARS

A WELL-SWEEP
FISHER TRAP

BURT CONKLIN ON
SHIRT-TAIL CREEK

LOUIE AT PILLSBURY

THE SPORTS LIKED TO HAVE THEIR
PICTURES TAKEN WITH LOUIE

LOUIE'S SUGARBUSH
IN OTTER VALLEY

that the limbs would bend down with their weight. There were beech nut slopes where they fed. Bill Wright would tell how Joe Cummings and Jerry Flansburg would get as many as three hundred and fifty in one day, using big nets on frames ten by thirty feet and pigeons with their eyes pricked out as decoys. They snapped their heads off, threw them into sacks and took them to Utica to sell. Bill Wright was one of the real oldtimers in Wilmurt and he knew how to get along with these lumberjacks.

After getting his pack which Wright had put in a safe place behind the bar, Louie walked up the road toward home. He stopped at Uncle Ed's place. Uncle Ed, in his apron, was standing in the doorway and behind him another face appeared, that of a lumberjack by the name of Tom Grimes.

"Hello, Louie," Tom shouted. "Louie th' thirteenth. Como se va, Bon Swa." Louie let his pack drop to the ground. "I know what'll fix you up, Louie. Come on inside here. Uncle Ed, two beers. There's nothing small about me, Louie, but my feet and my salary."

Uncle Ed opened up his ice-box and brought out the old brown pitcher. The beer was like hard cider. It did not sour. A horse and wagon drove up outside and Tom peered through the dirty cobwebby window where Uncle Ed had his "perfectly good" liquor license.

"That's Jim. Jim, the meat peddler. An' that's old Joe Van Cort and his goatee with him." Tom stretched his neck around the door-jamb and shouted through the open door. "Hey, you Jim. Ain't yo' pedlin' meat no more?"

"Hello Tom. Sure I'm pedlin' meat."

"Well if you're pedlin' meat what yo' got that bock beer sign on the seat for?"

Tom Grimes was not a real inhabitant of this north country but originally from New York City. He had fought in the Civil War and at rare times would tell how they were "slaughtered all around me" in the battle of Chancellorsville. Once, after tying his horse to a big burdock in front of Jack Ward's hotel at Gang Mills, he went inside to hear a loud-mouthed

129

lumberjack telling what a hero he had been in the Spanish American war. Tom, unable to take it any longer, went up to the young fellow. "Son," he said to him. "I fought in the Civil War, where the heroes, none of them come home. Yeah, sure, I come home, but the heroes, they all got killed." There was nothing funny about that. That was the other side of Tom, who was usually a "comical cuss", the quickest witted man in the woods. Tom worked for Sol. He was a handy man about the camps, a good carpenter on bunks and bolsters, sleighshoes and sleighs and snowplows. They made their sleighs right in the woods, hewed out the runners and ironed them. Tom was a reliable dam-tender and somewhat of a riverman.

Tom sang out again for old Ed. "We aint got no money, but we'll have some. We'll have money when pay day comes. Oh, Uncle Ed, will you give us some gin, we'll pay you when Sol comes in. Oh, fill up the old brown pitcher. That reminds me, Louie, of once when I was down in Utiky. I went in one of them high toned restaurants down there and a wide-eyed little waitress comes up to me an' starts jabbering away. My gosh, Louie, do you know, I swung around in that chair and I banged this old horny old fist o' mine down on that there table like that. Bang, and I told her a thing or two. She was scairt. Her eyes stuck right out. 'You think you're smart, don't yo', I yelled at her, 'but I'm tellin' you one thing. If I wanted such things I'd know enough to ask for 'em.' An' then I got up an' I walked right out of the place an' I went to a good eatin' house over in Deerfield where they know how to wait on lumberjacks."

Tom studied Louie's pack basket. "I be darned, Louie, if them ears on your gunnysack pack-cover there don't look just like Joe Van Cort's goatee whiskers."

The ears on the pack-cover? Slowly Louie remembered something, remembered how, just before leaving camp, he had tied some money in that pack-cover.

A rattling and grating of wheels and hoofs sounded in the stony driveway close to the doorway.

130

"Uncle Ed," Tom shouted. "Here's the stage. If yo' see Sol, you tell 'im I've went to Boonville to get me some lumberjack boots."

Louie took his jackknife and cut an ear off of his pack-cover and in another moment he was climbing up onto the stage seat beside Tom.

"What's goin' on here? This stage don't go up the West Crik."

"Utiky. Ba da holy feesh, Utiky." Louie answered.

The stage pulled away and near the Flansburg bridge they passed a big team driven by one of By Congdon's drivers with a heavy load of freight and baggage bound for Jocks.

"Hello there, Morey," Tom called out to the driver. "What yo' got? A load of silver dollars for Dut?"

The driver laughed a big hearty laugh for he too had been down at the Prospect Hotel that night when Dut Barber received the package of hard money from the express company.

"Yes sir, Louie," Tom said. "I never see so many in my life. Every man in Prospect except the parson was at the hotel that night pitching cartwheels."

The horses trotted over the sandy stretches near Grant, on through Gang Mills and over the plank road and it did not seem long with Tom talking all of the time before they were at Prospect.

Most lumberjacks, when they came out of the woods, started at the first bar in Wilmurt to fill up and the owner of the place wrote his name and the amount due him on the back of the check. When the lumberjack stopped at the different bars, new names and amounts were added until the check was used up and eventually turned in to the lumber company where each bar was credited with what was due it. Those lumberjacks who managed to get past the seven bars north of the Flansburg Bridge, got through to Prospect.

Louie went into the bar at Murphy's Hotel, the Adirondack House. Pushing right along with him was a gang of ten or twelve lumberjacks. Louie didn't know just where they had all come from all at once but Big Charley Teets, the blacksmith for jobber John Shiner, was talking to the lot of them:

"He asked me if I'd drink or fight. I told 'im I guessed I'd rather fight. I've walked around him for years," Charley was saying, "not 'cause I was afeared of 'im but 'cause I didn't want 'im to get one whale of a lickin'. I didn't keer 'bout givin' it to 'im but I guess now he'll stay out o' my way an' not be a botherin' me no more."

When they were all back again to the bar, Murphy announced, "There's goin' to be a Methodist donation tonight, boys, and I want you to show a little respect. Now 'spose we take up a collection and send it over to the church?"

"Sure," a lumberjack answered, "but say, better yet, I'll go get the parson." Out the door he went and soon came back with the pastor of the Methodist Church.

One river-beaten old log-driver stepped up in front of the pastor. "Hello Bill, old sport, have a drink."

"Oh no, boys, I don't drink."

"Don't drink! Listen to 'im. You an' me had lots of drinks together. Don't you remember me?"

"The man is right, men, but that was years ago," the parson began. The men listened. The talk was short but when he had finished the men knew that he was no "pig-yoker." The parson was a white-water man and the collection that was put into the hat, including a silver dollar from Louie, showed that the men were for him.

The next morning Louie walked over the hills to Utica. After selling jerky at the hotels in the city he visited a few of the bars most frequented by woodsmen. Woodsmen were always seen on the Utica streets. Utica, the city that had a nationwide reputation for rolling lumberjacks. Some hotels almost considered it their legitimate business to roll them. Thieves picked their pockets when they were drunk and left them lying in the gutter. When picked up by the police they were always too

132

drunk to remember who did it. And yet they came back for more.

At the bars, Louie heard them tell of the deaths of Ab Carnahan and Bud Smith told so many different ways that sometimes he had to say, "Ah was be dere."

And he also heard of another death up the old West Creek, that of Gene McBeth on Mill Creek near Nobleboro; how Gene had saved Eddie Watkins' life and lost his own. That was the way a lot of them went. One lumberjack was always ready to help another. "Saved him by 'is hair," a lumberjack would say, "an' 'twas a good thing he had long hair for I was a hangin' on to a mountain ash no bigger 'round than a file handle."

Gene McBeth was up on Mill Creek, so the story went. Sol had put some logs in up there and there was a jam. When the jam broke, Gene ran back to help Eddie get to shore. As Eddie jumped, the jam swung with fast boiling water, cutting off Gene. The logs turned in the current. Gene, going with them, jumped from one log to another. The last the men saw of him he was still on his feet, riding them, as he dropped out of sight around a bend in the stream.

They were sure that they would see him again, coming up along the shore, laughing as usual. But he didn't come and they looked for him among the rocks. Mill Creek joins West Creek in a stillwater, the last place to look.

The old blacksmith in the shop at Nobleboro tied on his heavy cowskin apron and went to work. He pumped the wheezy bellows late that night making grapples. "This is the thirteenth set I've made for just such purpose," he said as the sparks flew and he spit tobacco juice into the hot cinders. "And every one of them have found their man."

From midnight on through the cold small hours they rowed on the stillwater. At dawn, as the whole gang was about to go up to the hotel for breakfast, Fred Kaufman stepped back, "I'm goin' to paddle around a little more," he said and another fellow got into the stern with the grapples.

The others had just sat down to the table when Fred came running up the path to the hotel shouting that he had found him. All left their breakfasts and went down to the creek. They climbed out over the slippery logs on the shore and soon had Gene up onto the bank. They carried the body to the hotel and laid it on the horseblock. A leg was broken. The shin bones were sticking out through the pants.

The bartender, who had been listening, was glad he was a bartender.

On the street, Louie would pass the lumberjacks. "Hello there, Louie. Louie da boy."

He saw Tom Grimes walking up Genesee Street, throwing nickels to a gang of boys behind him. By the time they reached the Erie Canal bridge there was a mob of fifty or sixty boys around Tom, battling, piling up and tearing clothes.

Tom, another time, was playing bear. Tom had found a piece of rope and tied it to an acquaintance who was wearing a big black fur coat and they went along Genesee Street like a wandering trainer and his bear. At street corners Tom sang and the bear danced and climbed up lamp posts. Crowds gathered and blocked up store entrances until the cops appeared and broke it up.

Louie, after a few days, glad to head for home, walked across the tracks and bridge to Deerfield, and on up the Trenton turnpike, following the northern road over the hills to Prospect Station where he met the friendly drivers on the buckboards.

Billy Hughes said he was going in to Nobleboro that night with a load of French Canucks, lumberjacks for one of Sol Carnahan's jobs. So Louie hung around and waited. A carload of the Frenchmen arrived on the evening train and it was By Congdon's job to get them in to Sol. Four teams with long Welsh wagons were at the station when the train pulled in. They loaded the men in and took them up the creek that night. Billy Hughes, driver for By, went with one load and Louie rode on the driver's seat with Billy.

Lights shown in the houses as the town people drew the shades aside to peer out as the four wagons creaked noisily through the village street on the road to Gang Mills and Grant, the town that changed its name from "Booth" when Lincoln was shot.

Billy turned to Louie. "I heard Sol tell By, 'You get 'em in to Nobleboro an' I'll get 'em in the woods before daylight'."

The four teams all stayed on the plank road that night, paying their toll, not sneaking over onto the dirt road just before they came within sight of the toll-gate as Billy sometimes did.

They pulled into Nobleboro between three and four o'clock in the cool of the morning. As the men crawled and jumped and fell down off the wagons under the starlit open sky, Louie left them and headed off up the road. From the little hill beyond Mill Creek bridge he could hear their voices and see their firefly-like kerosene lanterns. Then on into the woods road where Louie's feet knew their way in the darkness under the trees. At Green Clearing it was gray dawn and Louie was feeling good for he was heading north, toward the trail up the old West Creek and home.

More Lumberjacks

Chapter Eleven

During the several years of lumbering along the West Creek Louie did not see very much of Newton Corners as he went out of the woods mostly to Jocks and to Nobleboro. When the creek was still open, he used his small canoe, going and coming on the big stillwaters, leaving it on the way out at the foot of the Swanson or First Stillwater.

The lumberjacks could ride a log, but even the cattiest of them could not ride this canoe. When they tried it on a Sunday for sport, one after another would be dumped into the icy water as it rolled over. Sometimes Louie would come along on his way in, usually full of liquor, and he would get into that little canoe, sit on the bottom, and with his legs stretched out in front of him, would paddle off unconcerned. The lumberjacks would watch him go and then just look at one another.

Louie became a familiar figure to the lumberjacks. He knew many of them and the jobbers, especially Sol Carnahan, the biggest jobber on the creek, having from four to six jobs going at once. He was a great Sol and he got a lot of work out of his men, yet they all said, "Never worked for a better man than Sol." Good men would not work for anyone but a good jobber, where they got better food and surer money. Second class jobbers had second-raters working for them.

In the summer Sol's men went into the woods about the first of June, cutting and taking it easy, not getting up until six in the morning and working until seven at night. In the busy winter months they had a two o'clock breakfast.

"Ye lads better be gettin' out," Boss Dan Casey would say and they would leave camp carrying a lot of torches like a bunch of soldiers. Every horse was out of the barn by three-thirty. The men were out in the woods sticking the torches in the snow doing half a day's work before it was daylight. Teams with lanterns hanging on the ends of the sleigh tongue, road monkeys with torches stuck in the snow alongside the hills, log rollers with a torch stuck in the snow on each side of the skidway.

Sol was right on the job. "Put 'em on, boys. Put 'em on. Get enough on there to sit on," he would shout. The sides of the loads would rise straight up. No good log roller ever tapered his load. They looked like a load of hay going down through the woods. The loads were heavy. They weighed around twelve tons in addition to nearly five hundred pounds of chain. To start them the teams would often have to saw back and forth until the frozen runners broke loose or iron bars would be used to break the hold of the ice. On a new snow the runners groaned and screeched like living things.

Toward the end of the day, when stopped at the skidways to load, the horses at times would be so tired that they would lie down in the road. The men got tired too but tired men working for Sol could sing, even on twenty-six dollars a month.

"Every Monday morning Sol Carnahan would say,
'Hitch up your teams, boys, get goin' on your way.'
And we'd say to Sol Carnahan, 'What road do we take?'

138

Sol would say, 'Just follow Burns and you can't make a mistake'."

The men worked long and hard hours for Sol. "Jumped into bed and turned over and got right up again." When one lumberjack complained about the nights being so short, Sol answered dryly, "And the days are mere nothings."

"Well, by Judas," the lumberjack came back at him, "I hang my pants on the bed-post when I turn in an' when I get up in the morning they're still swingin'."

A Frenchman at Bill Light's hotel at Northwood put it this way, "Ah come on de woods las' fall, on de night, an' ba gosh, ah come out me dees spring on de night also, an' dat camp, ah tol' you, ah nevaire wid daylight see wan tam."

But the men knew that Sol was one of them. They knew that he knew how to take part in the fun. When Sol had money he was free with it.

The boys from up the old West Creek were always glad to go out with Sol, not only because you couldn't spend any money when you were with him but because where Sol was, there was always a good time.

Once down in Utica Sol bought a bar for an hour and served free drinks to all. It was at the Bucket of Blood on Whitesboro Street at the corner of Hotel Street. Sol and a few of his woods friends were drinking at the bar. He hesitated for just one moment as his eyes scanned the rows of bottles on the shelves behind the bar before asking the bartender owner of the place, "Say, pardner, what'll you take for this goldurned bar for just one hour?"

The owner, expecting more to call Sol's bluff than to make a sale put the price at what he thought was high enough and answered brazenly, "Five hundred dollars."

"Good enough," Sol thundered. He slapped five hundred down and swung around and grabbed the first lumberjack he could get ahold of, got a good grip on him and threw him over the bar. "Get over there and get busy."

139

Lumberjacks crowded up and soon were elbowing with dere-
licts, and bums and their betters from the Utica streets as the
news flew around that the Bucket of Blood was serving free
drinks.

An old fellow who came in just out of curiosity to see what was
going on, said he didn't drink. "You smoke, don't you?" Sol
asked and gave him a box of cigars. Sol gave away everything in
sight and before the hour was up there was a crowd way out to
the sidewalk.

But Sol played square as always.

"That's all, boys, that's all. Time's up." And to the relieved
owner of the place, "When you get stocked up let me know and
I'll buy you out again."

Another time, it was at the Mansion House, which with its
long wide porches, stood on the corner of LaFayette Street and
Broadway in Utica. It was a place, mostly for farmers who
left their rigs in the low rambling Mansion House stables across
the street but along in the spring its peaceful countryfied atmosphere often got quite a jolt when lumberjacks from the north
country hit the town.

In the quiet carpeted "settin' room" a young lady was waiting
in a chair by a window for her farmer husband or boyfriend when
Sol Carnahan and a few of his stagged trousered Northwoods
crew peered in through the doorway before swaggering in with
their rough woods shoes. Sol, in the lead, moved toward the
piano and then, with a smile turned to the girl by the window.

"Give us a tune," he said.

"I don't belong here," she answered shyly.

Sol didn't see why she didn't belong there as much as he did;
but what difference did it make anyway.

"Well, bagawd, I do," he let her know in his loud outdoors
voice and with a couple of quick steps and a jump his feet landed
with a crescendo on the keyboard of the piano, his elbows out
just as though he was riding one of those big spruce logs through
Haskell's Rifts.

140

"Come on, boys, let's have a song."

The girl had disappeared but Sol stood there high above his lumberjacks. "What'll it be? 'Oh, The Jam on Gerry's Rock?' " The men gathered around the piano. "Come all ye true born shanty boys," they sang as Sol ran the scales in his calked boots. "They broke the jam on Gerry's Rock and received a watery grave!"

"What are you doing!" The astounded manager stood aghast in the doorway.

"I'm playin' the piano," Sol said. "I always play with my feet—'so manly, true and brave'——."

"You'll pay for that," the trembling manager shouted excitedly in a cracked voice.

"I'll buy you a new one," Sol shouted back, and went on with the song " 'and carried away six brave shanty boys and their foreman, young Monroe!' "

"I tell you you'll pay for that."

141

"I said, I'd buy you a new one."

And Sol did. The new piano was there inside of an hour and when they started to take out the old one Sol raised his hand.

"Hey, wait a minute. Wait a minute. That's mine. One more song." He leaped up onto the keyboard and danced up and down the keys.

" 'There's Mary Gallager, she's nice and fair,
She's as slim 'round the waist as a six year old mare.
She's neat, fair and handsome without any mistake,
And the boys, they all call her the belle of Trout Lake.'
"Take it away, boys. Take it away."

Yes, with Sol Carnahan, the boys always had a good rip snortin' time. One evening, at Foote's Hotel in Piseco, Sol surprised the men at the bar by riding horseback right in the front door. He rode right up to the bar and had a drink as the bartender petted the horse's nose.

At Wilmurt it cost Sol twenty-five dollars to cut off old George Wright's whiskers. Everyone knew of the old patriarch's beard and the old man thought well of it too as he had worn it for a good many years. Whenever Sol was feeling good around Wright's place he wanted to cut it off. He pestered the old fellow: "Here's twenty-five dollars. Give me the shears."

That was a lot of money for the old man and he could not help reaching for it. Sol took a grip on the whiskers with one hand and held the shears in the other.

"Here goes!" Sol's famous laugh, a laugh that "could be heard for a mile" echoed through the house. He had the whiskers and the old man had money for a necktie.

Louie worked some on the winter road at Bert Leavenworth's camp. This was the nearest camp to the West Canadas, the farthest camp back. It didn't have a piece of sawed timber in it; split balsam was used where boards were needed. Louie started working there when the first big snowstorm came, around Thanksgiving time. There was about a two-foot fall of snow and all the teams and sleighs turned out and went over the roads to pack it down. After the snow was packed, they put a Michigan snow-plow over it to even and true it up. This plow pushed the snow off on the sides and shaved the track down smooth, ready for the sprinkler. The sprinkler ran night and day, sometimes with heaters in the box to warm the water so that it would penetrate farther into the ice and snow. The clothes of the men working on this job froze into an icy coat of armor. After about two weeks of the sprinkler the real log hauling commenced. A smart lumberman never loaded his teams heavily until he had his roads in perfect condition. The roads were divided into sections and a "road monkey" was assigned to each to level up the track, fill in the soft spots and keep the hills well tended. Louie was day man or "road monkey" that winter spreading road hay for Bert Leavenworth. Bert gave him a horse that was troubled with galled shoulders which Louie sold to Trume Haskell sometime during the following summer.

With his horse and jumper, Louie, with a blanket about his knees and his hat pulled low on his head, rode over the many iced roads, stopping to sleep or to get a bite to eat at the lumber-camps along the way. Down between the high snow banks on both sides of the road, in zero weather, his breath freezing on his whiskers, the cold air biting his cheek-bones, the snow flying from the horse's big hoofs, Louie could see very little of the woods around him but now and then would spot a deer standing in the deep snow. The deer liked to follow the roads where it was easy going. When they started to yard, there were places where Louie could see ten or a dozen or more together. The horse needed no driving but guiding hands held the reins in case of an occasional pitch-hole or fallen tree branch. Louie's hands were warm inside of "fringe" mittens he had purchased at the company store. These mittens were all wool, knitted by hand by Kate VanCourt and her blind sister, "Blind Tom," as the natives of Wilmurt called her. They took orders all the year around, knitting continuously and selling to the jobbers or to the lumberjacks themselves for five dollars a pair. The mittens were called "buff" or "fringe" mittens and resembled the nap of a hooked rug. The men in the woods marveled at Blind Tom's handiness and swore she "never missed a stitch." And Louie's feet were warm too, inside of his rag moccasins that he had made himself from new wool cloth shaped to his feet and pulled over his shoe-pacs. Forty below was not uncommon but Louie was comfortable because he knew how.

Dave Walker, the "lumberjack horse-doctor," at George Welch's camp on Little Otter would look at the horse's shoulder whenever Louie stopped there. Dave "knew more about horse ailments than some college fellows who had taken a course in it." But Dave was more than that to the men, for they would send for him when anyone cut himself with an ax. Dave knew how to stop the bleeding.

Louie would often pass peddlers with packs on their backs, "outsiders" journeying through the woods visiting the lumber-camps, selling clothing, watches, jewelry, knives, mouth organs, thread and needles, bachelor buttons, pills, talcum powder for lice, gargle oil and the like. Sometimes they would try riding with Louie and would give him something from their pack to pay for the lift. Louie showed Trume a watch and chain that had been given to him by one of the peddlers.

"That watch," Trume laughed, "come with baking powder and the chain he stole off one of them boy's whistles."

And sometimes Louie just arrived at the lumbercamps in time for prayers. A good influence was Father Fitzgerald of Old Forge. He traveled through the woods stopping at all the camps. He reached them all; Jimmy Cosgrove's at the head of the First Stillwater, George Welch's on Little Otter; Bill Harvey's on Northrup, John Cole's near Mica, Eugene Abrams' between Sampson Bog and Spruce, and far away Bert Leavenworth's camp on Sampson Bog. At each camp he said prayers, sold five-dollar hospital cards and held raffles for the benefit of the church. Sometimes he would take in as much as seventy-five dollars on a briar pipe. He was known and liked all over the southern part of the woods and was always ready to loan a dollar to a broken lumberjack.

It paid Louie well to know all the bull cooks at the different camps. There was George Shields who had a perfect right to pride himself on his bread making, but he could move too when baking pancakes for thirty-five men. Nels Russell, with two chore boys, got away with nearly a barrel of flour a day. He'd cover a table fifteen feet long with fresh fried cakes and cookies. Theodore Genet was the best cook for "white tiger" and beans. He cooked beans to perfection twenty different ways. They were good, too, for an early winter morning breakfast when warmed up in a frying pan.

Johnny Leaf, a St. Regis Indian and Louie's neighbor at Mud Lake, was working for the lumber camps, supplying them with venison at from three to ten dollars a deer. When the camps were not so much in need of meat, Johnny would take whatever he could get.

"Dere's a wensen down dere," Johnny would tell the camp cook. "Ah guess ah wan' a frauer an' a sirp an' ah guess ah have a grease too." He would take his foodstuff and tell the cook where the deer was hanging nearby in the woods. One year the lumber company picked up beef cattle on the outside and drove them in to have meat for the winter.

When he kept the camps in meat for twenty-five dollars a month and found, he killed over fifty deer in one winter. He threw them on the nearest skidway where a team from the camp picked them up. Sometimes the carcass froze solid and the cook had to get the hide off the best he could as he cut it up for cooking, but plenty of hair went into the kettle and the Frenchmen ate it and liked it, eating the hide and hair right down with the rest of the stew. All camps had plenty of venison and at times a good mess of trout. On the South Indian in the spring a few men would go fishing on a Sunday and catch a washtubful of trout.

145

When Louie went down the West Creek with his horse and jumper, Trume Haskell took care of the horse for him until his return. Louie was seen at the bars around Nobleboro and Wilmurt among the lumberjacks there, but he never was really one of them. In a brawl Louie seemed to be unconcerned and at ease in the thick of it but not a part of it. Bill Wright, a big man with a big voice and a heavy hand, said that Louie was a "well mannered nice little fellow with curly hair." Louie quietly padded around in his rubber soles amid the noisy stomping of heavy lumberjack boots.

The Law

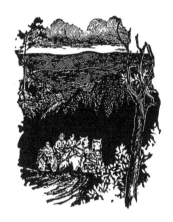

Chapter Twelve

Not only League members came to Louie's but others, some from as far as New York and Boston. These people from the east came in by way of Northville and the four horse tally-ho stage. The memories of one's first trip by this route would never be forgotten. Up the beautiful Sacandaga alongside the rushing river with the near steep and wooded mountains closely hemming in the valley.

Washburn was one of the stage drivers and there was Charlie Straight, who drove stage for over thirty years, and Oscar Benson, Martin Hayes, John Aird, Dick Shires and others. Among those who owned the stage lines were William Grinnell, Henry Eaton and Van Arnam.

The stage left Northville about ten-thirty after the arrival of the morning train from Fonda on the New York Central. Around noon they stopped at Hosley Hotel in Wells for dinner and to change horses and then on over the wooded hills arriving at Lake Pleasant about six o'clock. The next morning at seven o'clock the stage started on the return trip and they had to keep moving to cover the thirty-odd miles to Northville in time for the twelve o'clock outgoing train south.

Dick Shires was driving the tally-ho stage south one trip when just over the top of Guideboard Hill a storm broke and a cloud-burst let loose. Dick whipped his four horses into a wild run to get across the half dozen or more plank bridges just north of Wells before the flood hit them. Down Guideboard Hill, through Gilmantown, and past Charley Lake. It was a ride his passengers never forgot. The rushing water was swirling most up to the planks when he went over the bridges.

From New York City, the New York Central railroad sold roundtrip tickets through to Lake Pleasant. The stage ride was part of the ticket. From New York they took a sleeper so as to get the early morning train out of Fonda. Some took the Hudson River night boat and bought their rail and stage tickets at Albany.

The stage ride was one wonderful experience and for many it was the best part of their woods vacation. The tally-ho carried about twenty-five people. Some Saturdays there would be over a hundred people leaving Northville and, besides the regular stages, every horse and rig in the town would be needed to take them north to Speculator and Lake Pleasant.

In order to let Northville know just how many rigs they would have to get ready, Charley Straight would often take the six o'clock morning train to Fonda where he would check up on the people wanting to take the stage and telegraph back so that preparations could be made and the necessary rigs would be at the station when the train pulled into Northville at ten o'clock.

The stage ran all the year around. The mail had to get through and sometimes the drivers were late in getting home. In the spring when the ice broke up in the Sacandaga and the road near the stream would be blocked by floods and massive cakes of ice, the stage would have to find its way past on higher ground through farmers' lanes and fields. At least once each winter *The Gloversville Republican* would be sure to print an item about a big snowstorm and how Charlie Straight or Oscar Benson or someone else got through with the stage. It was tough going for the horses through drifts and blowing snow. It took a good man to drive that winter stage and they did get through.

Charlie Straight always carried about three hundred dollars in his pocket in silver and small bills to cash checks for people and to give silver to the stores in exchange for large bills. He would get around twenty-five cents each for these transactions. People along the road would give him lists of groceries to get for them, have him get some medicine that the baby was crying for or give him some message to deliver. The stage driver was the natives' handy man and friend.

Those going in to Louie's hired a rig to take them to Perkins Clearing a few miles north on the Indian Lake road. There a deal would be made with Isaiah Perkins who would transport the party and its gear with a span of mules and buckboard a couple of miles up the Old Military Road to Sled Harbor. This was an open grassy space in the forest at the start of such rough going that wheeled vehicles were useless and wood-shod sleds were needed. At times twenty or thirty old and new sleds were around about the little flat. The mules, unhitched from the buckboard, were now harnessed to a sled; half a ton of duffel or so was loaded on to it; and the party was quickly off on a sled road that led to Pillsbury and ended at Louie's Clearing on Big West. The men walked, the duffel rode, and the buckboard was left for Si to pick up on his return.

Usually Louie, if he knew the party was coming in, met them at his Pillsbury camp, or sometimes they picked him up at Newton Corners, and in no condition to ride a buckboard. He then would let himself be tied to the seat with ropes, so that he could not fall out when the vehicle bucked the holes and bumpy corduroy of the road to Sled Harbor.

The law bothered Louie very little. In summer months, in spring and fall, he knew who his parties were and in the dead of winter he was nearly snowed in and the law snowed out. The weather and his remoteness made him practically a law unto himself. In supplying himself with meat he broke some laws without a thought, and a feeling of what he considered his own rights made him break others. It was his way of life.

He was accused of many things he never did. Those who were arrested around Newton Corners for violation of the game laws would always complain that Louie was the worst violator of them all but that he was never caught and seldom even bothered.

"I kill one deer," they would say. "Louie kills fifty. Why don't you go after him?"

One spring, shortly before a large fishing party was expected to arrive at Louie's camp, the game warden, Emmett Lobdell of Northville, who was a conscientious worker, went in to the West Canada Lakes but kept himself out of sight and waited. He wore buckskins. He was hiding behind the boards propped up over the ice-hole when Louie came out of the camp with his gun. Lobdell saw him go back through the woods and later heard a shot over toward South Mountain and saw him return but with no sign of meat.

On the next day the two met. "Ah look for you," Louie told him. "Ah see sign, two, t'ree day. You hide in de ice-house dere. You no catch ol' Louie dat way. You look jus' lak deer, Meester Lobdell, w'en ah see you on de wood."

Another time Lobdell found Louie home, with a pot of venison cooking on the stove.

"The next time I see you out at the Corners, Louie, I'm going to arrest you."

"Nex' tam ah be dere," Louie agreed, and the next time that Louie was in town Lobdell did arrest him and put him in jail.

Louie's friend, Sam Noyes, was his lawyer and the trial came up at the Town of Wells with a jury of six good men. Two Rogers were on the jury and a Colby and others, just six good men, who, if they wanted meat, would probably go out and get it. "This written law," they said, "was made to protect game from those who shoot to sell. The little we kill will make no difference."

In answer to the question as to what he was shooting at when Lobdell heard him, Louie said he had shot a crane; as for the meat in the kettle he said it was hedgehog.

"Boil dem togedder an' see w'at dey taste lak," Louie said.

The people knew Louie was on trial for killing deer. Someone driving past shouted, "How's the case coming out?"

"Hell, look at the jury," was the answer.

Louie was acquitted.

Louie sledded many deerhides out of the woods. He got into his harness and hauled them out on his hand-sleigh, piled up like a load of tan bark, about a hundred to a load, which, if they were winter hides, would weigh about two hundred pounds. Winter skins were lighter weight, and although the regular price of nearly a dollar was paid for them, they made poor leather. A dealer in Newton Corners bought or gave Louie credit for many hundreds of skins. There was nothing illegal about selling or possessing deerhides, but the number of them that he brought out made people wonder where he got them all.

The game warden was also on the trail of the Indian, Johnny Leaf. Johnny was a good still hunter, as good as there was in the woods. His eye was keen and quick. He knew the life and movements of the deer, and it may be true, as Johnny said, that he never shot a deer running. He didn't have to. Game protector Lobdell was always going about the woods. From Leavenworth's camp on Sampson Bog he went across to Mud Lake where he saw a deer hanging in Johnny's woodshed. He was sure that Johnny would not move the deer but he figured he needed help, so he started at once for the outside.

Two days later, just before dark on this cold late spring day, Johnny and Louie were sitting in the latter's kitchen when suddenly a halloo was heard. They heard a team outside and then a knock at the door. It opened and there Lobdell stood; behind him Ike Kenwell who was a warden that year.

151

"Ba goshy, meester man," Johnny greeted them, "w'ere you go?"

"We're going to hole up right here tonight, Johnny."

Louie wondered what they had found out about now.

Kenwell pulled off his mittens. He gave Louie a reassuring glance to let him know that there was nothing for him to worry about.

"Ah tink," Johnny said as he got up and moved toward the door, "ah tink, Louie, ah got a leetle work to do."

"Just a minute, Johnny," Lobdell said.

"Ah gotta grease ma trap," Johnny insisted.

"Your traps can wait. Listen. About that deer hanging in your woodshed. You'll have to go out with us in the morning, Johnny."

"You damn good foolisher, but you no foolish me."

"Johnny," Ike Kenwell said, "we stopped at your camp and saw the deer you got hanging there. In the morning we'll be over after you. You better be there waiting for us, Johnny. You're going out with us."

Johnny opened the door and picked up his rifle which stood just outside, then stepped back standing in the open doorway. There was a moment of tension so quiet one could have heard the borer ticks working in the logs if one had noticed. Louie glanced toward the old Winchester hanging on the pegs over his bunk.

"Ah take ma fur," Johnny said.

"Sure," Kenwell spoke quickly. "Sure, Johnny, take your fur."

Johnny went out and slammed the door. They could hear his steps on the frosted leaves.

Sometimes Johnny, indignant and resentful when game wardens pressed him too closely, would in spite go back into the woods and shoot every deer he saw leaving them lay where they dropped. But on this next white frosty morning when Kenwell and Lobdell drove over to Mud Lake Dam,

Johnny was there with his pack of furs ready to go with them. They threw the deer in the sled. Lobdell said something about putting the handcuffs on Johnny but Kenwell said they would not be needed. Johnny was glad to be going out; but he preferred to walk rather than ride in the slam-bangin' old woodshod sled even with a deer to sit on; and walk he did.

At Sageville he was told to go and sell his furs. With "Hello Meester Man," and "Hello Meester Womern," he greeted the people whom he passed on the village street, and when he came back to the jail he was satisfied to wait for what was coming to him—good meals and a warm place to sleep.

There were three men who were as much a part of these cld North Woods as the very trees—Louie on the West Canada Lakes, Johnny Leaf living in his rough bark shack at Mud Lake Dam, they didn't keep Johnny long in the Sageville jail, and Frank Baker, once Barber's head guide, who had settled down by himself some distance north as caretaker for Chapin's camp on Beaver Lake.

Once a year Baker received from Chapin in Rochester three hundred and fifty dollars in crisp new five-dollar bills, which he kept in a black leather bag under his bunk, seldom finding it necessary to spend any of them. Chapin would send Baker anything he asked for. At the start of one cold winter he sent word to Chapin that he wanted twelve alarm clocks. Chapin must have wondered a bit but Baker got his twelve clocks and lined them up all in a row on a shelf by his bunk. His chunk stove was near the bunk too.

"What's the idea of all the alarm clocks?" asked a trapper, who had stopped in.

"Well," Baker replied, "it gets a little cool up here sometimes, so when I go to bed I set one clock for seven o'clock, the next one for eight o'clock and so on through the night. In that way they wake me up every hour and without getting up I just reach over and stick a piece of wood in the stove and the fire doesn't go out. Fact is, I got so used to them alarms I don't even wake

153

up any more but just stick the wood in the stove automatic like. Them clocks are all right."

When Louie and Baker and Johnny were apart, to hear them talk, one would think that they were deadly enemies just waiting for a chance to kill each other. To hear Johnny, he had it in for Louie; he was going to tell Louie this and tell Louie that, he was always ready to say, "Ah feex heem." But when they were all together, as happened when parties came to Louie's place, they were real friendly.

Louie knew all about Johnny's brave talk. One day they met in the woods.

"Hello Louie! Hello Louie!" Johnny called.

Louie had seen Johnny coming and had been watching him. "Dat mek me tink," Louie said when they came together. "You gonna keel me, Johnny?"

"No, Louie, no. Ba goshy, yo' s'pose man's gonna keel off hees bes' fren?"

Like old pals, they went back to camp together. But Johnny nearly shot Louie once thinking that he was a ghost. It was on a dull day in early fall. There was an inch or two of snow on the ground, a good tracking snow, and it was also hanging on to the limbs of the trees. Johnny was still-hunting on the east end of the West Creek range when he caught a glimpse of something moving. Something pure white. Johnny had heard of albino deer but this seemed to be walking like a man. A ghost! He watched an opening in the trees where he thought it would show up again; stood still, his gun ready and waiting. Soon there was a slight movement in the brush, and then who should step over the knoll right in front of Johnny but Louie. Johnny could not mistake that face but the outfit left him speechless.

"Ah fool 'em," Louie said.

Johnny lowered his gun. "Ba goshy," he whispered.

"Ah tink, Johnny, de red shirt, he fool 'em moche bettaire."

The sports, when they went out from Louie's place, left

154

many things behind them, such as good shirts and shoes and other things that Louie would get some real use of, but they also left some queer things such as a linen duster and a straw hat. These were what Louie now wore, trying to blend himself into the snow background.

Johnny shook his head. "Ah tink, Louie, ba gosh, you more craz as meester woodpecker."

Johnny and Louie were very unlike. Louie did not mind being alone, but Johnny often wanted companionship and would walk fifteen or twenty miles to see someone. A Frenchman, "Big Joe Cote," the pock-faced massive powerful fellow who packed loads from the tote-roads to the driving camps in the spring, came and lived with Johnny for a while until Johnny, who would much rather live alone, got tired of having him around and smoked him out. Joe should have known by the way Johnny hawked and spit and wielded the broom that it was time for him to move. Joe slept up in the loft of the shack, and in the middle of the night Johnny would get out of bed and close the damper and open the stove door. Joe, up above, with only one little hole about eight inches square in the peak for ventilation, was nearly suffocated before his great bulk, choking, watery eyed, half awake, would come crawling through the loft hole and down the ladder.

Johnny, back in bed, would mumble in his sleep. "W'at's da matter, Joe? Meester stove, he smoke?"

When this continued night after night Joe, at last, threw his few belongings into his pack and moved on.

In July 1898 the League had acquired title to the lumber company's property in Township 8 extending to Mud Lake. The aprons of Swanson and Mitchell dams were blown out lowering the level and bringing the water of the First and Second Stillwaters within their original banks. All lumbercamps in the valley, except the most substantial one at Swanson Dam, were destroyed. The old camp at Ferris Spring Hole was left intact but Johnny was put off and his shack at Mud Lake burned down. Louie did not drive Johnny off, nor had he "burnt him to hell out" as many supposed.

155

"Anyhow," Johnny said, "de likker, she too far."

He moved twenty-five miles down the West Creek into the abandoned old Morrison camp on the lower side of Frazier Brook at Seabury Stillwater.

He had a neighbor. On a high knoll across the brook, Nat Shepard lived in his neat little log camp with his wife and four children. Nat was a quiet fellow, sincere and honest in his love for the outdoors, a devout Christian at heart and industrious. He had dug a ditch following the contour of the hill until it joined the Frazier Brook about a quarter of a mile upstream bringing running water right to his camp door. He guided city sports fishing and hunting and would often take his children on camping trips. Once, with his two boys, after all three had prepared the evening meal over the open fire and were sitting in the shelter about to eat, Nat looked at them and said, "You know, I'd rather guide for you guys anyday than for the richest man I ever worked for."

Nat and Johnny fished and hunted together, good friends and companions. After a day of tramping through the woods they would stop at Nat's cabin where Nat would bring out a bottle and glasses. Johnny always raised his drink with the same old toast. "Meester Nott," he would say—he didn't seem to be able to pronounce Nat—"To you, Meester Nott, my good fren' as long as de water she ron downstream."

George Susie—that's the way the name sounded—was a Frenchman who stayed with Johnny. When Susie announced one bitter cold morning in early winter that he was going up around the Indian to check some traps Johnny advised him not to go but Susie had been lazy too long and wanted to get out so he put on his snowshoes and left. When he did not return that night Johnny was worried. If it had not been so cold and blustery he would have climbed up to the little camp on the hill and told Nat. But anyway, next morning he and Nat went to look for him. Nat knowing that Susie was not as young as he used to be, decided to take the hand-sleigh. They got an early start heading up the valley on snowshoes pulling the heavy home-made sleigh.

Just before dark the children plodded up the snowy trail expecting to meet them. As they climbed the hill and over Burnt Knoll they saw the two men coming toward them pulling the handsleigh. Something had happened to Susie!

When within hearing distance, Nat called, "You kids! Ward! Henry! Run for home as fast as you can and tell your mother to have some hot ginger tea ready when we get there."

They had found Susie lying in the trail exhausted and near frozen to death.

It was six miles to Nobleboro but Johnny went out and finally got word through to Doctor Longshore of Cold Brook who came to Nobleboro with horse and cutter and snowshoed in from there arriving at Johnny's camp before daylight but Old Susie was dead. The men pulled the body out to Nobleboro.

The following spring Nat and his family moved out to Wilmurt and as the lumber company was building a dam at the foot of Sea-bury Stillwater and about to make a muskrat out of Johnny he went up on the hill and lived in Nat's cabin.

Johnny had more company here than he ever had at Mud Lake. His old camp mate Big Joe Cote showed up again but was unable to keep up. He developed the tremors, went running wild in the nearby woods as though he weren't human and it took a searching party nearly a week to catch him. Johnny was always looking for liquor and he wanted it to "bite and scratch all the way down." "Yo' 'spose yo' gonna get any feesh on dat leetle bit of w'is'ey?" he would say as some sportsman handed him a quart.

A hunting party of eight came in to the Seabury, and with Johnny as their guide they went up farther and made their camp near Klock Flow on the Indian River. The party had considered Johnny's price of five dollars a day too high and Johnny, much against his will, had agreed to go with them for two. Each day they hunted; sometimes Johnny with a party, and sometimes he hunted alone. One of the hunters came over a rise of ground

157

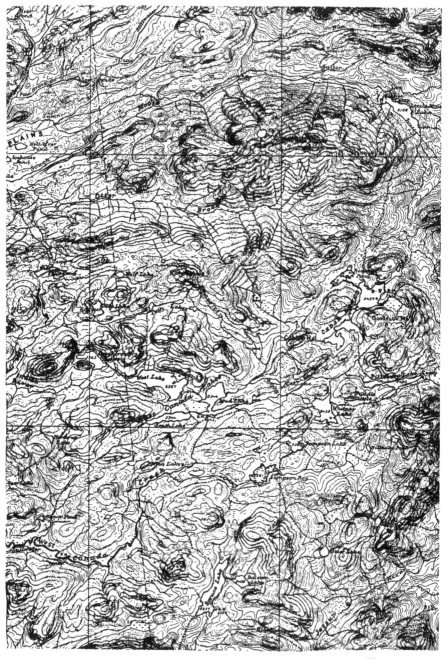

TODAY'S MAP

back from the alders on Split Rock Outlet and saw something black crawling along through the bushes. He thought it was a bear and pulled up his gun ready to shoot when he saw that it was a man on his hands and knees. The hunter hollered and Johnny Leaf stood.

"What are you crawling around like that for?" the hunter wanted to know. "I nearly shot you for a bear."

Johnny held up a finger and told him to be quiet as he was following a big buck.

The hunting was bad, It was the fourth day and they had but one puny little doe hanging up for camp meat. They raised Johnny to five dollars and told him to change their luck. The next morning Johnny went out alone and came back that afternoon with eight hearts. Eight nice bucks were hanging up in the woods.

Louie, on his way down the West Creek to Nobleboro, would often stop at Johnny's place, sometimes for over night. He was there on the fall evening when this hunting party returned to Johnny's camp where they would stay that night before going out of the woods. Johnny had cooked up a big pot of venison stew with carrots, potatoes and onions in it. It was good. They ate heartily until one hunter, when he forked in deep for another helping, pulled out a thoroughly cooked old woolen sock. Johnny tried his best to explain that it had fallen into the stew from a wire over the stove on which it had been hanging to dry, but some of the hunters had their doubts though not enough to spoil their appetites.

On another November evening three men were eating supper with Johnny when Louie came in. Johnny had been drinking and was not eating very much. "Hello, you ol' Louie," he said as he poured himself a cup of tea. The salt and the sugar on the table had thoughtlessly and innocently been put into similar white bowls, and Johnny, instead of sweetening his tea, put two spoonfuls of salt in it. He drank, choked and spit, and glared across the table at one of the men he believed to blame for the trick. He grabbed up the bread knife and went after him.

159

When Louie caught Johnny's arm Johnny probably thought he had gotten it into a bear trap. He quickly calmed down but was sullen and in the evening he walked out of the camp and did not come back. In an hour or so the four of them went out on the porch to take a look. They called a few times into the dark night but received no answer.

"Johnny, he no go far," Louie said.

"I'll bet he's gone to Nobleboro," someone said and they went to bed. Louie sat by the fire for a while before he too turned in, rolling into Johnny's bunk.

Johnny had not gone to Nobleboro. He had lain down on the ground nearby and pulled the leaves over him. In the night it snowed and when Louie came out in the little porch early in the morning he saw six or eight inches of new snow on the ground and to one side a queer looking white mound. He walked to it, kicked the snow off of it and out of the mess of snow and leaves and sticks Johnny aroused himself.

"You jus' lak wan ol' bear, you Johnny," Louie said.

"It's a good thing for Johnny," one of the men standing in the doorway said, "that a hard crust didn't form in the night."

Johnny went into the camp. As the liquor was all gone, he stirred a big spoonful of black pepper into a glass of warm water and drank it down.

160

LOUIE LIKED SNAKES

He made shelters for them, like
the one in the foreground

GANG MILLS
NOW HINCKLEY

Courtesy of Howard Thomas

SEABURY STILLWATER

WEST CANADA LAKE (BIG WEST)
A NICE CATCH

WEST CANADA LAKE
FROM MOUNTAIN

Photos by Bob Hughes, Amsterdam

SOUTH CANADA LAKE
BROOK TROUT LAKE

ON WOLF CREEK

Louie and Charles C. Henderson

Photo by Leland H. **Follett**

LOUIE DA BOY!

Photo by Leland H. Follett

JIM STURGES

STRONG BACKS AND
HEAVY PACKS LEAVING LOUIE'S

SOMETIMES EVEN A
PACK-MULE

Courtesy of Bob Hughes

JOHN HINES AND
NAT SHEPARD
Barber's guides

LOUIE'S CAMP IN 1913

CONSTRUCTING
THE FIREPLACE

INDIAN RIVER
AFTER THE BEAVER CAME

ISAIAH PERKINS' PLACE

ISAIAH PERKINS' PLACE
On the Indian Lake Road

LOUIE ON HIS WAY TO THE CORNERS

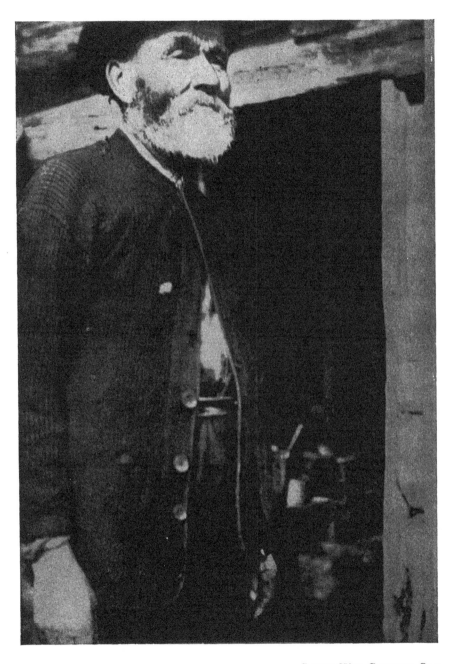

LOUIE WAS GETTING OLD

THEY CAME IN TO SEE IF
LOUIE WAS ALL RIGHT

BROOKS' HOTEL, SPECULATOR,
WHERE LOUIE DIED

THE FIREPLACE AROUND WHICH THE ROOM WAS NEVER BUILT
It is now standing at West Canada Lake, near the Forest Ranger's place,
preserved as Louie's monument

LOUIE'S SLED
The people of Speculator saw Louie pulling this sled heavily laden with furs
or supplies. It is now on exhibit at the Camp-of-the-Woods in Speculator

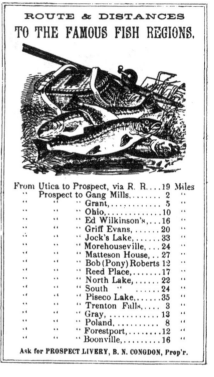

UTICAN URGES OLD LANDMARK BE PRESERVED

Plan to Destroy (Built by Hei Is Proteste

J.

A petition to the Stat tion Department not to an old stone fireplace French Lewey at the \ Lakes was contemplat Harvey L. Dunham, ...

Keep French Lewey's Fireplace

The idea of Harvey L. Dunham, Utica, that the old fireplace built by French Lewey, the hermit, at the West Canada Lakes should be saved is a good one.

French Lewey w
West Canada Lake
one. It is too bad
works of first set
have been gathe

FOR HONORING WOODSMA

State Plans to Reserve Firepl of 'Last Adirondack Pione

Special to THE NEW YORK TIMES

UTICA, Oct. 15.—A stone place built by French Louis, mit who lived a half centur deep forests of the West Lake region, may be pres his memory, according to received this week by I

State Will Let His ...ttler of the Fireplace Be His Memorial only

Special to THE NEW YORK TIMES

UTICA, Oct. 28—The State Con- y servation Department has decided en to preserve the old fireplace of rd- Louis Seymour, known throughout In Adirondacks as "French Lew- what ey," on West Canada Lakes, Sey- an- mour. who died some years ago, Lakes resided as a hermit in the most In- where accessible section of the Adiron- supply dacks for forty years. Although Seymour "lived off the country" regardless of game laws, number of Harvey L. Dunham hea... artist of Utica

BY CONGDON'S CARD

THE OLD FIREPLACE SAVED

Springtime in Otter Valley

Chapter Thirteen

In Otter Creek Valley, on the western slope of Falls Mountain, there is one of the finest stands of maple in the woods, over five thousand trees, tall and straight. Here about a mile north on the outlet of Falls Pond, Louie had his sugar bush of "mor'n a hundert trees." He erected three small log buildings roofed with large shakes: one not over four or five feet square in which to store the sap buckets, one where he made his sugar and syrup, and the third in which he lived. When the day's work was done, he slept on dried marsh grass in an old boat elevated somewhat off the floor. North of the West Canadas it could be like winter even in April, and the sides of the boat held the blankets close to his body and kept him warm.

His many sap buckets were about one foot square and six inches deep. They were made of birch bark cleverly folded and secured so firmly by birch skewers that scarcely a drop of sap leaked out. The best paper birch section was a few miles to the east of the Old Military Road and Manbury Mountain; and there he procured his bark.

He solved the problem of collecting the sap from the many trees by an ingenious system of troughs. These were made from straight-grained saplings gouged out by the ax. They were propped up and connected to form lines, which converged into a main stream, as tributary springs and brooks feed into a creek, and the sap flowed down and was caught in big troughs made of bark or hollowed out of twenty inch beech logs. Later he was able to get a few tubs or pails from lumber companies for such storage purpose. Such a collecting system was a necessity as his bark buckets did not hold a large quantity of sap, and he was saved the labor of dashing from the trees to the store troughs. Instead he merely dumped the buckets into the nearest trough line and let gravity take the sap down hill. He boiled it in crude sheet metal pans set on a rough stone arch over the fire; and the smoke could be seen from Kenwell's place at Indian Clearing.

Sometimes he threw a piece of fat bear-pork into the sap to keep it from boiling over. He collected empty bottles, of all sizes and shapes, and bottled the syrup to sell to the sports for about two dollars a bottle, regardless of whether it held a pint or a quart. He got dozens of pie-tins from the lumber camps in which to harden the sugar and stored a plentiful supply overhead in his main camp, using it instead of the granulated variety. Once he had twenty tubs on hand, nearly a half a ton, and there were times when it soured and had to be boiled up again. Later he had molds and made bars of sugar three or four inches square and about two feet long and would pile them up like cord wood. He made much more sugar than he could ever get rid of.

Besides syrup and sugar he had eggs for barter and sale. They were stored in tin boxes which he had gathered together. He seldom ate eggs, except in his cooking. One winter Pants Lawrence and four others from Newton Corners were hauling supplies on handsleighs in to Pillsbury and beyond, to their trap-line cabins. Louie told Pants that if he would pull a barrel of flour in to Pillsbury Lake for him, he would give him all the eggs he wanted. Pants pulled in the flour a good big six miles from Perkins. It was a troublesome top-heavy load on those steep climbs near Blue Ridge and frequently tipped over, but he got it at last to Louie's Pillsbury camp. Louie broke in the head and carried it in from there in lighter loads. Pants received six dozen eggs for the job.

Louie was a great believer in bear-oil to take internally or to rub on his skin or in his hair. He always had a pan of "bear-lard," as he called it, near the stove for his frying and cooking. Deer tallow would keep indefinitely but this bear-lard would soon get frowy. Up overhead hung large chunks of tallow, dark and dirty looking but pure white and clean inside, which he would cut into when needed for cooking or for making a new supply of short chunky tallow candles. Usually he went to bed at dark and got up with the dawn.

Louie improved the ice-house, logging up the sides a foot or so above the ground and closing in the ends with boards and a small door. He built a peaked roof with hooks at the top, on the ridge, so that he could open it out flat on hinges and catch a fall of the right kind of snow, thus saving him shoveling.

After supper and through the evenings, the sports, successful business and professional men, sat in the main room of the camp at the table, and on cool evenings around the low three foot chunk stove, or tilted back in their chairs against the log walls, and talked in the dim light of candles and kerosene lamps. They played cards, read old papers and *Forest and Stream* magazines, joked and told stories. Louie would be in his kitchen or standing apart from them, perhaps leaning against the post beside the doorway between the big room and the kitchen, watching and listening to the yarn swapping with a little smile and saying nothing. When a good one was told someone would turn and say, "What do you think of that one, Louie?" and Louie would hardly move but his eyes would brighten and he might just shake his head and say, quickly, " 'Taint so."

If bottles were uncorked, Louie always refused a drink. He never drank whiskey in camp. He would not touch it, no more than he would yell and holler in the woods.

163

On spring evenings before they turned in for the night a smudge pail would often be carried through the camp to drive out or stupefy the punkies and mosquitoes that had managed to sneak in during the day. In the fishing season a smudge pail was usually burning somewhere about the camp, generally on the hard dirt just off the porch.

One fishing sport, a wholesale cigar dealer, brought cigars. An empty cigar box on the table gave the party the idea of making a fiddle.

Louie became greatly interested. "What you mek heem out of? You mek eet a fiddle was good for play?"

With the cigar box, some fine split balsam and a few pieces of fish line the fiddle was made. A tune was actually played on it and Louie was tickled pink. For years after the fiddle hung on the wall, a prized possession.

"Did you hear about your old friend, Tom Grimes?" an architect asked. "He shot a fellow up at Piseco Lake and now he's serving time in Dannemora."

"Tom Grimes, the lumberjack who worked for Sol Carnahan down the West Creek?" the Western Union manager asked.

"Yes. Near the head of Piseco Lake Tom forgot himself and through jealousy over a woman he up and shot the eye out of a man named Briggs. Really, the bullet just nicked the bridge of Briggs' nose, and Briggs ran with his hands over his face and fell headlong onto a woodpile and poked his eye out. That's the way I heard it. Anyway, Tom was sent to Dannemora Prison for three years. He still had his old humor with him when he was being taken away."

"Leave it to Tom Grimes."

"In that queer rasping voice of his, he says, 'I got one job now, boys, that no one can finagle away from me, not for three years anyway.'"

"Did you hear what happened to him when he got to Dannemora?" the brewer from Utica asked. "At Dannemora they asked what his trade was on the outside, and he said, 'Carpenter', so they gave him a job next morning building a coffin for a fellow who Tom said was an old lumberjack friend of his."

A doctor looked up from an old copy of a Gloversville newspaper. "He was a great boy, Tom was. One time when he was working as time-keeper at one of Sol's camps, Tom's figures did not agree with the claims that the men put in. When Sol wanted to know why it was, Tom explained that the men better be paid their demands, for the cook had burnt up the flour sack with all the figures on it."

"I saw him just once," the lawyer stopped his game of solitaire to tell. "We came on to him when we were going out of the woods at Flat Rock on the Jocks Lake road. I had heard how Tom used to carry his whiskey into the woods in a jug riding on a stick on his shoulder. Well, this time the jug had slid off the stick and Tom was down on all fours lapping it up from little pools in the rock. 'Hurry up, you guys' he yelled at us, 'don't let all this go to waste.' "

"That's Tom, all right," said another of the party. "He always had his medicine with him when going into the woods."

"There's a lot of stories told about Tom. Pete Wurz, who runs the Farmer's Hotel just across the river in Deerfield, tells how Tom once came into Pete's hotel and wanted a room. He told Pete that he did not want to be rolled, that he wanted a room all by himself with a lock on the door. Pete gave him just what he asked for but the next morning when Tom came down, he was fit to be tied. Someone had rolled him in the night. Pete knew something about woodsmen and he led Tom up to his room and questioned him. They searched and found a hole in the corner of the pillow and in the feathers was Tom's wallet and the roll of bills."

The judge, who had been turning the pages of *Forest and Stream* magazine, joined in. "Maybe that was Tom but I heard the same story about someone else. It's a good story, anyway. I stopped at Tom's place once when he was tending dam at Frazier Clearing. We wanted to wash our hands for dinner and someone says, 'Where's the wash basin, Tom?' "

"Wash basin?" Tom asked, "wash basin? Hold on, boys. By gosh, I'm glad yo' spoke of it. I'm bakin' bread in it."

"Listen to this," the judge who was looking at the old *Forest and Stream* magazines spoke up, "this is from the March first issue, 1890—'from the best evidence obtainable there is a pack of wolves which have been in the vicinity of West Canada Lakes for several years. Louis Seymour, a French Canadian guide has made his home, winter and summer, on the shores of "Big West." He has frequently met the pack and has numerous stories to tell of their destruction of deer and other game, but what he seems to care most about is the impossibility of his keeping a dog but a little while as the wolves kill them off. At first he thought his dogs got lost by following deer into other territory, and then they were taken in by guides finding them but now he firmly believes that the five dogs lost each year 1888 and 1889 were killed by wolves'—How about that, Louie?"

"Dat's right. I 'member de wolf, he keel off eight-nine-ten dog dat tam."

"Say," the lawyer changed the subject. "A friend of mine, who travels on the road, was stopping at a hotel, I think it was down to Elmira, it doesn't matter, but anyway, whom do you think he saw? He was sitting in the lobby when a man working in the hotel started cleaning the cuspidors. It was Barber of Jocks Lake. He was feeling all right. He was working at the hotel for his board and lodging."

"He's dead."

"Who's dead?"

"Barber. Didn't you know it? He died in the Poor House in Penn Yan. Old cronies passed the hat to save him from Potter's Field. He's buried in the Forest Hill Cemetery in Utica."

"My gosh, those that stand high have a long ways to fall."

"Queer how old Kettle Jones went. He was leaving Honnedaga for Snyder Lake. George Wandover saw him go and called to him. 'Hey, Kettle, that's not the trail.' 'I know it. I'll hit it,'

Kettle hollered back.' That was the last anyone ever saw of him."

"That was John R. Jones."

"Wasn't John R. Jones, Kettle Jones?"

"No. Kettle was Owen Jones, John R. was Dingle-dangle."

These fishermen enjoyed their evenings at Louie's as much as they enjoyed their fishing.

But Louie actually paid very little attention to many of the sports who came in. He would often get up in the morning, cook his breakfast and go out without a word to anyone. He might be away all day or perhaps not return for a day or two. Sometimes when he came back he would go up the ladder, and one could hear him up overhead prying the cover off the tin can where he kept his maps. After a little time he would be heard shoving the can back again into its safe dark place under the eaves where no one would disturb it.

Or seemingly in the middle of the night, one might hear him moving around starting his fire and getting his breakfast, and in the cold half-light before dawn, gently slipping out the door and down the path to the boat. As those in camp pulled the blankets closer for more sleep, they could hear the fading clank of Louie's oarlocks as he rowed away into the low white mists. He would troll on the big sand-bar until about ten o'clock. When the fishing was exceptionally good he would catch a dozen or so nice lakers, a pack basket full. A few years had made a difference; they ran smaller now.

One party at Louie's was not catching any trout. On the third day when they wanted some fish to take out, they asked Louie, "Where do you catch trout around here anyway? We just can't go back without a mess of trout after coming way in here to the West Canada country."

"Ah go git dem," Louie said.

The fishermen gathered up their tackle ready to start. This was fine.

167

"Ah go, me," Louie said and he went alone. In a few hours he was back. There was the old twinkle in his eye as he slowly raised the lid of the basket and let them peek in at a mess of beautiful speckles, enough for them to take out and not be ashamed of.

"Where did you get them," they all wanted to know.

"Ah git dem," Louie answered quietly. "Ah got a place."

The sports had faith in Louie. One party who was coming in from the other side, sent word to Jim Sturgis at Newton Corners to get word to Louie to have him meet them at a designated place on the edge of the Big Plains on a certain day. They hired a pack horse and guide at Fourth Lake on the Fulton Chain and went south to the Plains where the guide left them. While they were building a fire, they heard a rustle in the bushes and out came Louie. He could be depended on. They went with him and stayed that night at his sugarbush camp near Otter Creek. There were no bunks; they slept on marsh hay, Louie in the flat-bottom boat, the others on the ground.

On the way, Louie showed them a metal-lined box that had been used to transport beaver when Harry Radford, publisher of the magazine *Woods and Waters,* first brought beaver into the woods and liberated them. There were many signs of beaver around Otter Creek and Louie expressed his hope that they would come to West Canada.

It was a year or two after this that the same party were at Louie's for some early spring fishing. They had been away all day and, when they returned at night, they noticed that Louie did not seem so friendly. Something was the matter.

"What's the trouble, Louie? Something gone wrong?"

"Ah feel pretty bad."

"Sick?"

"No seek. On Mud Lak ah see somting sweem. Ah tink he ees otter an' ah shoot heem. Ah get de boat an' ah peek heem oup an' he was beeg beaver. For long tam ah wan' for dem come an' firs' wan dat come, ol' fool me, ah shoot heem." On

168

the next day Louie showed them a big beaver where he had thrown it behind a log.

Louie was always busy. It would take him but five or ten minutes to eat, then away he would go. If he sat down, it would be only a minute or two before he would be up again and doing something or other. If ever he was tired, he didn't show it. When the camp was settling at one corner, he cut spruce poles thirty or forty feet long and using these as prys, he raised the whole camp alone and fixed the foundation. But with all his tireless nature, with all his ambition, he never cut out any trails. On the trail to Mud Lake, which he followed almost daily, he walked around the same fallen tops and stepped over the same down timber for years with never a thought of chopping them out.

He could keep going at the same pace all day while his guests tired and their knees gave out. They watched him with wonder as he shouldered his pack or pulled on the oars or stepped quickly at the end of the day. Was he tireless? "That's what woods life does to a man," these city sports said to one another.

"Aren't you afraid to stay way back here all alone all winter, afraid that you might get sick?" Louie was asked.

"Ma fren', ah tol' you, when ol' Louie die he come back."

He really believed it. "Ol' Louie, he come back."

As the sports flocked to the woods, names of places were often changed. Names of certain sections were being dropped. One never heard now of "John Brown's Tract" or "The Reserve." You didn't hear about Indian Clearing. Now it was always "The Big Plains." In this southern part of the woods where the country had belonged more to the natives, "The Adirondacks" was at last taking the place of "The North Woods." Sageville Courthouse was now called Lake Pleasant, Round Lake was changed to Sacandaga and Newton Corners became Speculator.

There were other changes, too. A group of sportsmen headed by several prominent men who had been in to Louie's decided to monopolize this country for themselves. An exclusive club was to be formed with Louie's site for the lodge headquarters. A big lumberman and a Buffalo lawyer, who had a camp at Honnedaga, proceeded to purchase the famous five-thousand-acre tract of virgin timber which included the West Canada Lakes.

The club was organized and actually paid Louie for his buildings and boats and it was known to be only a matter of time, and not a very long time either, before Louie would have to go. He had been told that he was going to be put off but he had heard that before. He didn't think he ever would be. He felt that everything would go on the same as it always had. A party, who had come in to draw up the preliminary plans for the grounds and new club house, asked Louie if he would get them a bite to eat. Louie reached down to the ground outside the kitchen door, picked up an old sock lying there, gave the cold grease in the frying pan a quick swipe and went to the cooking.

The club plans progressed. It was named the "Altamont Club" and metal signs were posted on all of the lakes and trails. "No Trespassing." "No Hunting or Fishing."

"What strange object is this which I behold," a hunter guest of Louie's exclaimed when he saw the sign for the first time before him on the trail, "Incongruous in its staring whiteness of fresh paint and black lettering, its straightness of lines and abrupt irregularity amid the soft tints and graceful curves of this sylvan scene. As I live! A trespass sign!" Up came the old Winchester. The signs made good targets for the outsiders as well as for the natives. They aroused much feeling and resentment as at this time throughout the state the movement was growing for a state park, where the state forest could remain wild and the property of the people forever.

Those who had financial interests in the country were afraid of what Louie might do if they actually put him off. They were afraid of fires. Weeks went by and Louie stayed on. Months passed and Louie was still there and the new club house was no nearer being built.

He went with a party as their guide to Swanson Pond to prospect around an old mica mine. They looked it over and planned to stake out a claim but found later that a claim had been staked and filed for years. The party brought out samples

170

of queer looking whitish rock, and Louie got quite a kick out of seeing these men fill up their packs with heavy stones.

The smell of frozen ferns was in the air and then came wet snow and dark days. The hunting season passed as usual and Louie went out to the Corners for supplies. On his return trip the winds changed and the cold rain turned to snow and Louie was glad to get back again to his camp, for now winter had set in and he knew that the outside world would not bother him for awhile. The long winter also passed and at last sap began to flow and again he made his syrup and sugar. Spring came, the birds began to arrive and the ice honeycombed and went out of the lakes and ponds. When the witch-hopple was in blossom and the low places rang with the chorus of the spring peepers, members of the new club came in to fish and Louie heard talk that he did not understand. And then one fine spring day an official of the lumber company came to the camp.

"What are you going to do, Louie?" he asked.

Louie wondered if the time had come. "Ah dunno me. Mebbe stay. Mebbe ah go."

"Well, Louie, you don't have to go. You can stay here just as long as you want to."

The club couldn't get satisfactory lease or title so they had given up. The state apparently had acquired the underlying title but the land was subject to an outstanding timber cutting right granted to A. Dallas Wait who assigned his cutting right to the Union Bag and Paper Co. of Hudson Falls. Now the five thousand acres of beautiful timberland was controlled by the big lumber company.

At the time that the change was made they discussed the best way to care for Louie. The timber was valuable and the fact that there had been no fires in all the time that Louie had been in there, spoke well. They felt too that the safest way now, the sanest thing to do, would be to let him stay. So a sort of agreement was drawn up allowing Louie to stay at his camp after the lumber company had taken possession. Trume Haskell took the papers in and got Louie's mark, and Louie was given six hundred dollars and was to act as fire warden. "Ba cripe," Louie knew all the time that they wouldn't put him off. One trip to the settlements of course separated him from the six hundred.

He had all the freedom now that one could ask for, as much as any owner of the land. He was getting out some logs when he saw two men with packs come out on the lakeshore across the bay and he recognized one of them as his old friend Isaac Kenwell. He put in a boat and rowed to meet them. Kenwell and an ambitious official of the lumber company, after one night at a cabin on Cedar River Flow, had tramped on to the West Canadas. As the sun rose higher in the sky they had slowed down, and between flies and warm weather, they rested often before they came out upon the lake and saw Louie coming toward them with a boat.

The young executive went fishing while Kenwell and Louie proceeded to put up the tent. They were in the tent preparing a soft fragrant balsam browse bed and Kenwell was saying, "We've got to give him a good soft bed, Louie," when they heard the fisherman returning.

"Who cut these trees?" he was shouting.

"They're balsam. We cut 'em for the bed," Kenwell told him. "If we hadn't cut these trees you wouldn't have a bed to sleep on."

Next morning when the two landed at the clearing where Louie was working, they saw newly cut peeled spruce logs there. The official from down the river could hardly control himself.

"What's all this? Who cut these logs?"

"Louie," Kenwell said.

"Louie! Louie! Who the hell is this Louie? Who said he could cut these trees?"

"I did."

The young man stared at Kenwell. "I'll have to report this, Mister Kenwell."

"Who dat fellow?" Louie asked as the zealous officer poked around the pile of logs inspecting the damage.

172

"Oh, he's just one of my bosses."

"Ba cripe, Louie don' lak eet de boss lak dat."

This young boss was a neat type and some of the things that he saw around Louie's back door did not improve his appetite; however they used his stove and they did let him do some cooking for them.

"How you want de egg?" Louie asked.

"Boiled," Kenwell said quickly.

"Boiled!" the young man shouted as he caught the significance. He turned his head and out of the corner of his eye he saw a movement of something between the logs. "What's that? Oh, it's a snake!" he cried as he jumped up from the table.

Kenwell saw it. "Look, Louie, there's a big snake in the logs."

"Dat's ma fren'," Louie said and went on boiling the eggs.

He allowed no one to harm these two big snakes that shared his camp. They cleaned up the scraps and crumbs about the place and in the summer they were Louie's farm hands in his potatoe vines to pay for their board and keep. Someone had named them "Darby" and "Joan". Once Joan spent some time in the flour barrel in Louie's effort to rid the flour of little white worms that had appeared there.

Along in February a lumberjack stopped at the Haskell Place. A trapper had told him that French Louie was ailing, lying in his bunk and coughing, and had not been out of his camp for several days. Trume Haskell, who would do anything to help Louie, got word at once to Doctor George C. Morey down at Grant, one of the old-fashioned kind who was always ready to go, even as far as the West Canadas. He was "no good for walking patients," they said, but all right if one was awful sick. When farmers saw his fast team coming along the road, they looked out for their dogs as the doctor always carried a revolver and several times he had proven himself to be a good shot when dogs ran biting at the horses' feet. The doctor drove to Haskell's where he and Trume took a fresh pair of horses and drove on the

173

packed ice lumber roads as far as Welch's lumbercamp near North-rup. Here they left their team in the lunbercamp barn and snow-shoed across to Louie's.

They found him on the verge of pneumonia. Doctor Morey gave the camp a good airing out, enlivened the fire and brought two pails of fresh water from the spring. They watched over Louie and enjoyed being there and ate brook trout caught through the ice.

After five days the doctor and Trume began to think of the return trip. "You'll be all right now, Louie," they assured him.

The doctor wanted no fee, did not want to take anything, said that he was having a good time, that he and Trume were having a vacation, but Louie thought differently and dug into a kind of a safe deposit box and made the Doctor take fifty dollars.

During the last evening Louie became more talkative and he told them of what happened to bring on the sickness.

On a bitter cold day he was returning from Wolf Lake to his camp and was crossing Brook Trout Lake with a load of steel traps on his back. These lakes are spring fed and have places that never freeze thick enough to support a man. When part way across he walked on to such thin ice. He felt the ice gave way beneath his heels and threw off the pack of traps just as he broke through into the black water. He was heavily dressed. He held on to the edge which kept breaking away but managed to keep his head above the water. At last, where the ice was thicker, he reached over as far as he could and when his mittens froze to the ice, was able to pull himself out. There was no time to spare. The cold wind was freezing him as he doggedly made his way to the narrow strip of land between Brook Trout and Big West and on to his camp. With great effort he started his fire and got out of the frozen clothes. But it had done something to him. He was shaking all over. He crawled into his bunk. Some time later, Louie didn't know just how long it had been, a trapper stopped in and after he left Louie had found a pile of fine split wood beside the stove and plenty of good cooked food on the table. Louie didn't eat much but kept the fire going and had hot tea, and he knew all the time while he lay there alone on his bunk that he was a very sick man. He thought he was a goner. And then there were voices outside and stomping of feet. The door opened and out of the cold Trume and the doctor had come in. Everything was all right.

"When you broke through the ice there, Louie," the doctor said, "I don't see how you ever got out of that hole. How did you ever get out of that water?"

The old twinkle was back in Louie's eye. He was himself again.

"Ba cripe, ol' Louie get out jus' sam lak otter."

"You're a tough old bird, Louie," Trume told him, "but did you know that your old friend Johnny was dead?"

"Johnny? Dead?"

And Trume told Louie how Johnny passed out, how he was killed in a fight last fall. Johnny was out on a four- or five-day drunk and might have been feeling a little ugly. At a hotel in Wilmurt he got mixed up in a lumberjack party and ran his face into a pair of calked shoes. It appeared that Johnny was practically trampled to death, that nearly every bone in his body was broken, and from this and other causes, such as falling or being pushed down stairs, Johnny died. Between Wright's and the Iron Bridge he was buried in a little white fenced town graveyard by the side of the road, alongside a lumberjack named Dan McNeil who had been found dead in a mud hole up back of Green Clearing.

"Johnny, he come back," Louie said.

Trume and the doctor slipped on their snowshoes and were ready to go.

"Good bye, Louie. Take care of yourself."

"Ma fren' ah tank you. Ahm glad for see you. Dat tam mos' mek eet de finish for ol' Louie."

"By the way, Louie, whatever became of Kate, the old dog?"

Louie shook his head slowly and looked at the doctor with an inquiring glance.

"She hunt no more. Ol' Kate dog, she get too ol'." As though listening he turned his head toward the window and the woods side of the clearing now buried in snow. "Long tam ol' Kate dog is sleep out dere."

She had become blind and feeble, so deaf she couldn't hear when Louie talked to her and one evening when he knew her condition was hopeless he took his gun and mercifully ended it. He wrapped the body in a blanket and carried it in an old pack basket out back of the garden. There he buried "Ol' Kate dog."

For a few moments they were very still for fear of saying the wrong thing.

"So long," Trume said, "so long Louie."

Hidden Camps

Chapter Fourteen

Of Louie's many outlying camps the one at Elbow Stillwater on the Indian was his most finished and showed the best of his workmanship. It was located "almost opposite, crosscountry, from where Yale Brook comes into the Cobblestone." The only tools used were an auger, a knife and an ax. It was nearly all enclosed but a partly opened end took out the smoke from an inside hearth. The door was one piece of split spruce, twenty-two inches wide, five and a half feet high and about an even two inches thick. The latch was whittled out and fastened with wooden pins. No nails were used, just boring and pegging. The hinges on which the door swung were wood, with wooden pins turning in wooden sockets, all cut out of spruce, and these hinges were pinned to the door with wooden pegs. The floor was smooth and made of two-inch split planks. The side walls were chinked with moss and the roof was made of what was called "scoops". Logs were split and hewed out to resemble a trough. The first row was laid closely together with the trough side up, the second row was placed over them with the trough side down and overlapping the first row. This was a strong, watertight roof, but only an experienced man could make it.

The camp at Louie Stillwater on the Indian was small and different from Louie's other camps in that it was completely enclosed and had a fireplace at one end. It was set back in thick spruce, well hidden as he approached it different ways so as to avoid making a path. Directly back of it a cold spring brook flowed between shaded mossy rocks.

This camp was most comfortable. It had a solid smooth plank floor, clean and white. The base of the fireplace, where the cooking was done, was of rock but the flue was composed of split balsam logs, halved with the flat side in. The fire and sparks would draw up this wooden chimney and yet the balsam did not seem to catch fire. In the fireplace was a crude grate made of lumbercamp iron, and kettles hung on hooks to one side. There were a woods-made table and one solid chair with an easy back, the style found in all his camps. The seat of the chair was a heavy piece of split birch.

The bed was a deerskin stretched between two poles, with the hair on the top side. The edges of the skin had been treated to remove the hair and the hide was thonged and laced to the side poles. "Babishe," Louie called it. He had a small canoe and paddle hidden nearby, and to one side of the camp several steel bear traps could usually be seen, each one weighing over twenty pounds.

No one ever molested these camps. "Ah got trap set for bear." So Louie warned any who gave signs of getting too familiar in his territory.

Louie liked this Indian River country. It was here that he made his jerked venison. Eight or ten deer were needed for one pack basket load of jerked meat as he got no more than ten or twelve pounds from one deer. After the "jerky" had dried it was much lighter. He only jerked the hams and saddle and a little of the best meat in the shoulder.

His method of jerking was to chop down a large tree so that the limbs would hold the trunk up four or five feet from the ground. The top side of the trunk was trimmed off flat and hollowed out. In this he put his strips of venison rubbed with salt, to stay for about a day and a night. Then a long smoky fire was built between two green beech logs and fed with beech chips. The smoke rose through a sapling and twig frame on which the strips of venison were now laid. Beech chips were used because they were sweet; never spruce which would give the meat a bitter sour taste.

There were different ways to jerk venison. Will Light, who ran the hotel at Northwood, cooked his venison over a bed of coals. First he cut the meat into strips eight or nine inches long and stacked them inside the hide—layer of salt, layer of meat, layer of salt. "Let it take up the salt. Take all it can over night." Then he washed off the surplus salt and hung the meat on green sticks over a bed of hardwood maple coals, three or four inches above the coals. When coals ashed over, he put on a stick the size of your finger. "Don't let the flames reach the meat. Throw on a spoonful of water to dampen them down. And when the meat stops drippin' she's done." Other men, after rubbing salt and pepper well into the strips of venison would let them hang in the open air, not in the sun, no smoke, no heat, until they were well dried. But however it was made, it was all "jerky."

Tim Crowley, the gum picker from Piseco, once came upon Frank Baker in the woods. Baker was jerking venison and had nine deer hanging up. Another time, Tim saw three fellows, including Birdie Haskell, each pulling a deerskin bag filled with jerked venison through the snow toward Morehouseville. They were making a track in the snow two feet deep. Jerky on the outside brought a dollar and a half or two dollars a pound, but woodsmen as a rule did not sell much of it as it was too valuable to themselves for food.

There was very little lumbering on the West Creek now. The lumbermen had gone leaving behind the litter of slash and roads through the woods for the sports to come in on. From early spring fishing until after the hunting season in the fall, the woods seemed to Louie to be full of outsiders.

There were three camps on Big West and guides were bringing in large parties and carrying out big loads of fish. Other native woodsmen made a regular business of netting the spring-holes and carried out pack-baskets full of speckled trout to sell at the hotels; combined parties of twelve or fifteen or more had wire screen cages alongside their boats to put their fish in until they were ready to leave, when Perkins or Sam Lawrence came in with mules and sled and hauled out the fish. There was much envy and jealousy between some of these outside guides and Louie.

Large parties came to Louie's. During the season the camp was filled up, every bed taken and some sleeping on the floor; and they took out shameful catches of fish. Many came up the West Creek but most came in by way of Pillsbury and had their duffel hauled in and the fish hauled out. The best of sportsmen were there too and saw what was happening. They deplored the use of nets and regretted the change that was taking place.

This wasteful destruction was kept up just as long as quantities of fish could be taken, until the exceptionally good fishing was a thing of the past. The day soon came when speckles were no longer "packed like sardines" in Brook Trout Lake and in Big West lakers or "salmon" as they were called were seldom caught. The number of fishermen became less; the ones who continued to come were those who really enjoyed the woods more than the pounds that they took out.

On one rare occasion a fisherman came into Louie's kitchen with a nice large lake trout.

"Ba gosh, dey bite," Louie exclaimed surprised, and took his pole and went fishing. Times had changed.

When crossing a slippery spillway on an old lumberdam on the Indian River, Louie fell and injured his shoulder. After a few painful days around camp alone, he started for the outside to find one of his doctor friends, a Doctor Earl Fuller, who lived somewhere in Utica. It was a long trip before he arrived in the city where he walked a mile or more over hard sidewalks stepping off onto the softer dirt and grass whenever he could paying no attention to the offices of many other doctors and questioning few whom he passed on the streets. At last he reached the house and cautiously went up onto the porch and knocked. A boy opened the door. Louie was dressed in heavy woods clothing, worn and dirty, and his whiskers were roughly trimmed.

"De doctor, he leev here?" Louie asked.

"No," the boy answered and was somewhat disturbed when Louie stepped inside. "No. Yes, the doctor lives here but he's out. It will probably be hours before he returns."

"Ah wait for heem."

The boy, who was the doctor's son, was quite concerned about having this man in the office but soon began talking with the suspicious character and then found out that he was none other than "French Louie." The young lad promptly recognized the name from the many stories he had heard, as there was never a gathering of any of those who visited the West Canada Lakes without French Louie being thoroughly discussed, with new angles of his amazing character forever appearing. The boy's attitude changed from that of a guardian of the office property to one who was anxious to become a friend of this patient and in his effort to make Louie comfortable, found out how he had injured his arm and how he had come out of the woods, all of the way from camp, to find the one man whom he believed could make it well.

Eventually Doctor Fuller returned and was surprised when he saw who was waiting for him. He examined Louie and found a dislocated shoulder. As this dislocation had existed for four or five days, the shoulder was badly swollen and inflamed. The doctor immediately said hospital and an anesthetic, but Louie did not like the sound of it. He was not going to go there.

So he stretched out on the floor of the office. The son was given the job of helping to hold him steady while the father took hold of the arm and, wedging his heel into the armpit, proceeded to set the shoulder. The pain was terrific but Louie just ground his teeth. When the ordeal was over they helped him on with his coat and tried to convince him that he must stay for dinner and spend the night so that he could again be examined in the morning; but Louie was too uncomfortable in these surroundings. He appreciated what was done for him but he was relieved and glad when the time came for him to be on his way. Back again at West Canada, the shoulder did not interfere with his going about the same as ever, doing a good job in giving the sports something to remember and talk about when they returned to their city homes.

On a warm fall evening Louie was heading for Mud Lake to float for deer, and with him were two of his regular guests.

Mud Lake in any weather, any season, was a lonesome wildness. Great blue herons, hell divers and loons crying at sunset, and at night deer splashing in the lily pads, gave one the feeling of being "way back in." Many times at dusk in the summer a dozen or fifteen deer or more could be seen at one time. With its muddy shore line and grassy flats, it was a good place to jack for deer.

Although the state in 1897 had made jacking and killing deer in water illegal they still had a floating season which thus far had been exceptionally poor and very few deer had been killed in front of the jack. The weather had been cold and damp and deer had not come down to the water as much as usual. But on this night the air was muggy and close. The two followed Louie over the trail by the dim light of a small kerosene lantern with a smoky chimney.

At the shore of the lake the night seemed blacker than ever. Louie set the lantern down on the ground and pushed the boat into the water. One of the sports wore rubber; that was all right, but Louie reached into the bow of the boat and found some gunny sacks for the other to tie around his leather boots. He did not object to their talking in low tones when floating for deer but he insisted that they wear rubber or wrap burlap around their heavy boots.

They pushed off and floated quietly through the darkness with no sound save the very faint gurgle from Louie's well manipulated paddle. There was a smell in the air of mud and marsh. There was no glow in the sky, no sign of the black shoulder of some wooded mountain.

They lit the jack and when the light shown near the boat they appeared to be in about eight or ten inches of water, but when Louie tried the depth with his paddle he pushed it down out of sight with no resistance. The man in the bow handled the jack and all watched for the white reflection of deer's eyes.

Then in the seemingly impenetrable curtain ahead of them a dull soft light rose from the water and lit up the side of a great rock back on the shore.

Louie, as if talking to himself, said, "No deer tonight."

A voice answered a little above a whisper. "Did you see that light? There's no place for anyone to camp in there."

A low smothered "Ha ha ha ha" came to them over the water.

"What was that?"

Louie turned the boat. Even in the blackness he knew where he was as they peered for signs of the shore in the path of the jack.

"We go to camp," Louie said as the boat grated on the bottom. "No deer tonight."

Along the trail they said nothing to each other until one ventured, "What do you mean, Louie, no deer tonight? Why no deer tonight?"

"No deer, de lak, she work."

"Work? Oh yes, sure, but can't you jack deer when the lake is working?"

"No deer w'en she work."

"What was that sound like someone laughing. Did you hear that, Louie?"

"Dat was de bubble. She come oup, plop, plop, polp. De light on de rock, ah see heem plaintee tam. Ah was be tol' me dat was de phosphor."

"Well, Louie, that is the first time I ever saw that. Boy, what a night." And they both felt different now as they went along the trail, after a new experience.

Not only fishermen and hunters, but treasure seekers as well hired Louie to guide them. Near the head of Cedar Lakes, when the lumbermen were cleaning the channel of the river for log driving, they found solid red birch logs which had been used in the building of the old military road in 1817. Near Racquette Lake this road joined the road from Boonville that had been put through the same year. Very little sign of the old road remained when the lumbermen appeared decades later. In places a trace of it could be detected in the woods where earth embankments had been dug away, and by looking up into the trees one could sometimes even notice a difference in the timber.

A party came to Louie's with copies of papers that told of an iron cannon full of coin buried on the old road and that gave directions for locating it by describing certain markings on rocks. Louie went with this party as guide, and for several days they followed the old route and in many places where they knew from vague indications that they were on it, they found rocks with queer markings, but they found no gold in those hills.

On the way to the Cedars this party saw one of Louie's outlying shelters. On an old logging-road was an abandoned water-tank road sprinkler. It was tipped over on its side, and Louie crawled in and out of it through the partly boarded up opening for filling it with water. In it was a bunk, a makeshift stove and stovepipe. It was a tight camp although small. "Queer fellow," the treasure hunters said of Louie.

Two young city sports at Louie's were somewhat startled to see Louie quickly reach for his shotgun and kill a robin in his potato patch.

"They're awful nice birds, Louie, you ought not to shoot them."

"Dey pull up all de fish worms," Louie answered.

It was noticed that after every fishing trip Louie would go out back to the bushes at the edge of his garden, reach down for something and in a moment or two replace it and return to camp. Curiosity was aroused. There was no reason for Louie to be hitting the bottle on the sly, although no one had ever known him to drink in camp anything worse than a swig from the Worcestershire bottle. One of the sports investigated and found a jug. He pulled the cork, expecting a strong liquor smell, but the whiff he got was terrible, "enough to knock a man down." The jug contained decomposed fish guts. Louie used the resulting oil in making a trapping lure. When one knew Louie better his actions were not so queer.

A fishing party was in with Bill Courtney at his Spruce Lake camp and were lazing comfortably before the fire about lamp-lighting time when Bill looked out of the window and said, "Here comes Louie."

Louie came in, in his double breasted shirt and baggy trousers, with a rope about his waist and cords about his pantlegs just above his low rubber pacs. "Hello, Bill," he said simply and sat down. He did not want anything to eat. When it came time to turn in, Bill offered him a bunk but Louie said he would just sit there by the fire. He sat there all night. When it began to get gray in the morning, Bill saw Louie get up to go and raised himself in his bunk to tell him to stay and have some bacon and pancakes; but no, Louie could not wait. He left as quietly as he had come in the night before.

"Guess he don't like our company," one of the party said as he rubbed the sleep out of his eyes.

"Oh, Louie's all right," Bill said. "That's just his way."

Good Times

Chapter Fifteen

Louie, for the most part, let his guests find their own pleasures, but when he did take them fishing or hunting and they told him what a wonderful time they had, he would say, "Ah have good tam, sam' lak you."

He seldom knew from one day to the next what he was going to do. If you wanted him to take you somewhere, or go with you, you had to use tact. He was an independent old cuss. That's why he didn't like the lumbering jobs. Sometimes a sport would lay money down on the table trying to make an agreement and Louie would push it back. He did not want to be tied down, but still there were exceptions, for if Louie said he would be at a certain place he would be there.

But you couldn't come right out and ask him to take you anywhere. That didn't go at all. He never liked to plan ahead and certainly did not like to have anyone plan for him. If you wanted to go to some particular place you could just casually say that you would like to go there sometime and perhaps ask about a trail, "What side of the brook does the trail go, Louie?" The chances are that in the evening Louie would say, "We go to Deep Lake in da morning," if that was the place you had been talking about, and that would be the signal for you to get your stuff together for Louie would be getting up at daylight.

Louie's idea of traveling, you might say, was something like a bear; if he wanted to go somewhere, he just went. There would be times when he would skirt a swamp, but in the woods, he just went. He didn't give the appearance of hurrying but he covered a lot of ground and you had to keep moving, sometimes you had to trot, to keep right behind him.

"Don't fight da brush," he would say and sort of sift through, sometimes sideways, even go through witch-hopple so easily. He wouldn't bull through it. And he would always travel light too on these fishing trips, not carrying much—a half-ax, a small pack, a little grub. Of course he did have stores of grub cached around the woods.

You would be going through the woods with him when all of a sudden he would say, "ah got traps down here," and he'd take a little side trip to check up on some traps he had hidden. He would kneel down beside a big log, push sticks and leaves aside, and usually too he would check up on a bottle of sulphur matches.

When sleeping out in the woods, he'd have tea and supper early. Then he'd throw up a little brush shelter by putting up a couple of sticks with browse on top and shingling some browse in for a bed. He would be up in the morning at daylight.

No one would suspect Louie of hollering when he was in the woods, but he did holler at camp one night just before dark.

He and a sport were in front of the West Canada camp when out on the lake a loon called.

"What the devil was that?" the sportsman exclaimed, who had never heard a loon before. And then Louie hollered and the sport jumped three feet and the loon answered and Louie and the loon hollered back and forth. It's safe to say that around back of camp one couldn't have told which one was the imitation.

Louie didn't take up with everyone. You'd see people come in to Louie's camp, people he knew, and set their packs down and start taking the stuff out. Strangers would leave their packs on or take them down easy as Louie sized them up. Sometimes he would tell them that there wasn't any room and they would have to travel on and make camp somewhere in the woods.

One bright June morning Louie was rowing alongside the meadows on the east side of Cedar Lake. Small white clouds dotted a deep blue sky. A light breeze rippled the blue water. Gulls were sitting on the rocks out in the lake. The air was clear, crisp and clean. Louie rested on his oars and his narrow eyes looked long at smoke rising from the log driver's camp at the outlet. It was all right for anyone to use the place but these outsiders sometimes did queer things. He turned his boat and went down to see who they were anyway.

Louie was like a fire-warden without pay. He questioned the three boys who were there. They resented it, thought it was none of Louie's business. And when they asked Louie about trails they disagreed with his answers. They had been reading maps and were too smart.

That evening, back at Pillsbury, Louie stood in his doorway with a frying pan in his hand and watched a tired young lad with a heavy pack come plodding across the clearing.

"What's da matter, Bub, you lost?"

The boy let his pack to the ground. "No, I'm not lost, I'm here, but where is Cedar Lake?"

That amused Louie. He chuckled. He knew that when the

189

boy had come to the fork in the trail way back at the foot of Blue Ridge, he had taken the left hand trail when he should have kept right. During a good supper the boy told how his party had gone on a day or two ahead and he had come in alone to find them. They were camping on Cedar Lake.

"I hope I can find them tomorrow," the boy said.

Before turning in for the night Louie said, "In da mornin' we go to Cedar Lake."

Next morning they took a boat and went down Pillsbury. Louie let the boy row. A duck with little ones swam along just ahead and the boy pulled harder on the oars to catch up with them.

Louie laughed, "Yo can't catch em."

They landed and tied the boat and took Louie's short cut over a little hog's back and were over there in half an hour. At Cedar Lake Louie took the oars and they soon were at the log driver's camp. The fellows there were surprised to see the missing member of their party coming in from that direction with Louie. When the welcoming was over Louie motioned to the boy and told him he'd be over after him in the morning and take him fishing. That was something all right.

For a week, until the grub gave out, Louie came over from Pillsbury every morning, and took the boy exploring and fishing in different places. The best place was around the rocky islands where the gulls nested. They would sit there in the boat and look down in the clear water and see those big trout, some of them eighteen and twenty inches long. They dangled the worms right in front of them and caught some nice ones.

They trolled with Louie's hand-made spoons. For Louie made his own trolling spoons, patterned after old spoons that he had way back on Lewey Lake, spoons made by Buell of Whitehall and Chapman of Glens Falls.

They went over to Wakely Flow and fished where Buell Brook comes in. They went to Spectacle Ponds and to Louie's

West Canada camp. They slept out off toward Kitty Cobble, and Louie showed the boy the ledges and caves. The boy was a little scared sleeping out but Louie told him there was nothing to worry about in the woods; it was in the city where you looked for trouble.

He gave the boy lessons in woodcraft, showed him animal signs and places where he had trapped. Once he sniffed the air and said there were deer near, said he could smell them, smelled "like a wet horse blanket." He impressed on the boy that when traveling through the woods to keep the lay of the land in mind and how the streams ran, told him to step over a log, not to step up on to it. "You get bad fall off a log." If you're going somewhere and want to come back blaze the opposite side of the tree. Simple enough to Louie.

The boy showed Louie his hunting knife and asked if it was a good one. "Any knife that'll cut bacon," Louie told him, "is a good huntin' knife." When asked where is the best place to hit a bear to kill him, Louie said, "Hit 'im anywhere. Get 'im down. Den dere's plaintee tam to do yo' fancy shoot."

Soon the vacation was over and the boy realized that it had been just a streak of luck when he had taken that left turn to Pillsbury on the way in. But he came back year after year and became one of Louie's regulars.

That same summer when he was back for a short trip of a few days he was told when he arrived by stage at Newton Corners that French Louie was in town and was "drunker than a boiled owl."

There were more ways than one at such times that Louie was short changed and Pants Lawrence got some liquor too that he did not pay for. Louie would get a room and go to bed half drunk. Just about the time he was ready for bed he'd pound on the floor for a bottle of liquor which was taken up to him. He'd take a drink and go to sleep and soon afterwards Pants would go up and take the nearly filled bottle away and place an empty one in its place. The next morning Louie would pound on the floor for another bottle.

191

The boy saw Louie who paid no attention to him. With no desire now to go in the woods, he got a room in the same hotel where Louie was with the idea of taking the stage back home in the morning.

There was the usual loud talking around the bar but Louie didn't know the boy from a bump on a log so the boy went to bed. After midnight he was awakened by what sounded like hoot owls in front of the hotel. He heard Louie's voice and got up and pulled his clothes on and went down to see.

Louie was getting his pack out from behind the bar. The first thing he always did when he first hit town was to buy his provisions and pack his pack all ready to go and put it behind the bar. Now around one or two o'clock in the morning he shouldered the pack and went out the door, the boy behind him. The town was asleep, or trying to be. Before he went off the porch, he raised his head and the hoot owl again broke the stillness of the night.

"Come on, Bub," he said, the first sign of recognition.

At the top of Page's Hill they turned and looked back. As they stood there in the dark Louie sent the tremulous unearthly call of the loon out over the town. The townspeople heard it and knew it came from Page's Hill, rolled over in their beds, thankful that Louie's spree was over.

Eyes became accustomed to the night, finding the way over corduroy on the old road through the woods to Sled Harbor. Louie had his shirt tied in back and hanging down, and the boy hung on to his shirt-tail as they staggered up the rocks and across the brooks over Blue Ridge.

They stayed at the Pillsbury camp and the boy was thrilled by an old panther skin thrown across a bench and he held the cannon ball in his hand, the three inch cast iron cannon ball that Louie had found on the old Military Road near Miami Stream.

They took a boat down Pillsbury to a spring-hole where they could see the mass of black trout on the bottom, but the trout wouldn't bite. Louie cut a sapling and trimmed it, leaving a bunch of branches and leaves on the tip. He put it down into the spring-hole and churned up the bottom and they left it and then after a while they came back and the boy soon had a mess of trout to take home.

One year about the first of June two young boys came past Pillsbury and on past the Puddle-hole on their way to fishing in Whitney. They had a twenty-two rifle. Soon after the boys had gone out of the woods, Louie went over the trail and when he came back he was really mad. Those fellows had killed a deer near the Puddle-hole, probably just to see if they could kill it with a twenty-two rifle, and let it lay. Louie wouldn't have found it if he hadn't smelled it. If they had come back and told Louie about it so the meat wouldn't be wasted, it would have been all right. He wasn't mad because they had killed the deer; he simply did not like the idea of wasting that meat.

William L. Ralph, M.D., a noted ornithologist, came regularly to the West Canadas. Charley Haskell, better known as "Birdie" because he was forever collecting birds' eggs, was his guide. Birdie would even travel on snowshoes looking for the nests and eggs of birds around the West Canadas in the winter time, the great horned owl and the Canada jay or whiskey jack down from the Canadian spruces. These jays, like chunky French Canadians, were no more afraid of the weather than they were of the lumberjacks. They sat on their eggs before the winter snows began to melt, even when the temperature was thirty below. Collectors and museums bought eggs from Birdie Haskell.

Doctor Ralph wanted a camp of his own on West Canada, so Birdie with the aid of Louie built a small log camp for him on the north shore of Big West near Sucker Brook, where the trail leaves for Twin Lakes. It was low and massive and roofed with lapping split balsam logs. A short man could just stand up in it.

The ornithologist had heard of the eagles that nested north of Piseco Lake near T Lake Falls. About fifteen miles south of the West Canada Lake, the outlet of T Lake drops five hundred

193

feet over a cliff into the south branch of the West Creek. Just south of the falls is a high bare ledge that is known as Eagle Cliff from the number of eagles that are said to nest there.

The bird man engaged Birdie Haskell to get a clutch of eggs for him. By taking a few turns of a rope around a tree at the top of the ledge and with Louie managing the rope, Birdie was slowly lowered to the shelf where the nests were. The birds, defending their nests, fiercely attacked Birdie. He was badly cut on the arms and neck. A pair of birds tormented Louie on the cliff above, but he stuck to his job and soon had Birdie up again with the eggs. They were well paid for their work although the eggs, when they were delivered to Doctor Ralph, turned out to be those of the duck hawk. Dr. Ralph gave a twenty-year collection of birds' eggs and nests to the Smithsonian Institution.

Louie dressed the same summer and winter. Often he wore a Ballard mackinaw in summer which he said, if it kept the cold out it would keep the heat out. He had a short wide foot and wore shoe pacs the year around. But what one had to look at a second time was a pair of Malone pants that Louie had patched so much that it is certain they could have stood alone like a couple of lengths of stove pipe. He not only patched them but when the knees wore out he wore them the other way around with the seat in front. He never sat down much. They probably were half worn out when he got them from some lumberjack.

But what a man he was with the crudest tools he had to work with. He made benches and chairs, of course, but he also made latches and hinges of wood. He made wonderful paddles with an ax and draw-shave. His stretcher boards of white pine for his skins had to be just so. He had barrels of them up stairs in his Pillsbury camp. In his West Canada camp he built stairs in place of the original ladder and the smooth split treads were mortised in perfectly.

Perhaps one reason that Louie was able to do such good work was because he had plenty of time and very few things ever bothered him. He never fretted. Rain never irked him.

194

If he was wet or if he was dry, it was all the same to him. Once on the Moose River the party was looking for a place to get across, looking for stones to step on, but Louie walked right in up to his waist and was soon on the other side. The two fishermen with him wasted time looking up and down the stream. At last, jumping from one rock to another, they both fell in and when they got across they were just as wet as Louie.

There was one thing that bothered everyone. Punkies. Sometimes Louie's face would be so swollen that his eyes would be just slits. But even punkies did not interfere with Louie's good times.

The Last Portage

Chapter Sixteen

It pleased Louie to have at his camp men who really enjoyed being in the woods; and he now planned to enlarge his place to accommodate the increasing number of fishermen and hunters, by building a large room on the south side of the camp. There was to be a great stone fireplace at the end of the room around which his guests could gather and swap their stories instead of sitting around the dark old chunk stove.

The fireplace was the first job; and Louie went to work and was very particular in choosing the stones. Some he brought in his boat from around the lake. The large capping stone lay on the shore not too far away. He made a log stone-boat and got the stone on it and, when Perkins came in with his mules, had him pull it up to where the fireplace was to be. When the lake froze over, he hauled one choice stone across on the ice on his sled. It was heavy hard work, and Louie was not as young as he was once, yet toiling all alone he laid up the whole fireplace, even to placing the large stone on top, which he did with the help of prys and blocking and a big tripod and tackle.

As more people were now coming to the West Canadas who did not stay at Louie's a strong feeling was growing against him among certain campers and guides. The word was passed around that if Louie could be "run out of there," the fishing and hunting would be better for everyone. They were riled to think that he, with his large parties, was always there, making a business of cleaning out the fish and killing all the deer. And now he was planning to build a larger camp. This was going too far. Something ought to be done!

Something was done. Agitation was started with the lumber company who owned the land to get him out; but right away good sportsmen, all the way from Boonville to Indian Lake, from one side of the North Woods to the other, raised their voices to have him stay. And they were heard. They told of fires he had put out and of lost persons he had found. Isaac Kenwell spoke out:

"A man like him! Listen to me! He's a valuable man. For thirty or forty years he's kept watch for fire and saved the timber in there. I've seen timber across the whole of Canada, but I've never seen a nicer stand than the spruce around Jimmy Pond, and Louie saved that for us. There hasn't been a bad fire in all the time that he's been in there. Sports came in fishing on the West Creek and started small fires. As soon as Louie saw smoke down river or anywhere else, and he was watching for it, he would pack his pails and shovel and go. He'd go ten miles down the West Creek and work several days putting out fires. No sir! Don't put him off! He's a valuable man in there and you must not put him out."

Louie retaliated too. When he heard that certain guides with a large fishing party were coming to Big West, he cleaned the brook trout out of the spring holes before they arrived—more than he could use—and he now put his rifle in the boat when going fishing. One day out on the lake he shot a hell diver just to prove to a party in another boat that his aim was still good.

"Ba da holy feesh! Who own dees lak!"

A year had passed since he started the fireplace. The work had gone slowly, for whenever he was ready to go ahead with the camp, his side bothered him so that he could not continue. He complained of a pain in his ribs and of a rash breaking out on his skin. It hurt him even to carry a pack. He, Louie, had to stop and rest on the trail! Most of the time he stayed around the camp. Although he still set traps, the lines were short and near by where he could easily watch them. He could not wander and climb over the wooded slopes looking for deer the way he used to and there was no Kate dog to drive the deer in so he placed a set gun with a cord stretched across the runway. He had to have meat. He never went as far as the Moose River and he took very few trips to his cabins on the Indian. Tired. The sports came in and made themselves at home as they always had. Louie took it slower and easier than he really wanted to. He could not understand why he felt that way. But, anyway, he was now a member of the New York State Forest Fire Field Force and he had a paper to show it. A fire warden appointed by the state! That helped some.

Jim Wadsworth, guiding a party from the League, stopped at Louie's. There were two women in the party. On their way in they had stayed one night at the Ferris Camp at the head of the Little Stillwater. They didn't get much sleep. Jim had heard a rustling overhead and grabbed a paddle as a big porcupine came down and waddled out through the doorway. The logs of the camp were full of snakes. Next day on the trail, with a boat on his shoulders, Jim had to stop to take a porcupine quill out of his leg. They stayed at Louie's two days, and Louie took a real pleasure in showing the women the interesting things about the camp. In the spring he had put some sap in a barrel to ferment and now he gave them a drink of his sap-beer, which they thought pretty good.

"Jeem," Louie said, "ma rheumatiz ees bad. You do good here. Ah sell you ma rights. Ah sell dem cheap. Yo' mek more monee, plaintee more as me."

Jim couldn't see Louie living anywhere else. "You better stay right here," he told him.

Jim brought Louie some news from the outside: how they had put a monument on Johnny Leaf's grave. Johnny had friends even among the sheriffs. A former sheriff had taken up a collection; many contributed and a stone was put on Johnny's grave. And Tom Grimes back from Dannemora. Tom was riding along the road past where Johnny's buried and he reached over and pulled up the team and jumped out and ran to Johnny's grave with a quart bottle of liquor in his hand. He got down on the grave and shouted:

" 'Hello there, Johnny. Are you dry? Johnny! Johnny! Come up here an' have a drink.' But of course Johnny didn't come up so Tom had to drink alone. 'You old reprobate,' Tom yelled. 'You're gettin' awful independent, aint yo', since yo' got a lot of your own.' "

Yes, Jim told Louie, from then on, not just on Decoration Day but any time, a traveler driving along the road between Wilmurt and Nobleboro would very likely see Johnny's grave decorated with a few empty bottles.

Louie did not go down the West Creek any more but he went out to the Corners about twice a year. At the hotels, where he stopped, he was more of an attraction than ever. Because of the attention he needed and because he never again would bring out the heavy packs of furs, one hotel man did say that he would rather see the devil walking in than to see Louie coming, but even though he did use his own boots for chamber pots and walked out of the place in bare feet shouting "Louie da boy!" the hotels were in business to make money and Louie was a great trade drawer. "Better than a bear on a chain," another hotel keeper put it.

"Did you have a good time, Louie?" he was asked when he

returned to the Corners after a Fourth of July celebration at Northville.

"Ba gar," he told them, "ah ride dat merry-gone-round all day."

It was the first real merry-go-round that Louie had ever seen and he rode every animal on it.

On this trip to Northville he saw one of those new chugging automobiles coming toward him. "By cracky, here comes a wagon afoot!" an old fellow next to Louie exclaimed as the driver maneuvered his skittish team past the "confounded contraption." But Louie had seen them before down in "Utiky."

He took his time going back into the woods, stopping for several days at Pillsbury on the way. He wasn't feeling just right. Back again at West Canada, it looked as though he never would get that new room built around his stone fireplace.

Ernest Brooks, as jobber, was lumbering near West Canada with three camps, one at Whitney, one between Mud and Cedar, and one at the head of Mud, which was about a mile from Louie. Brooks thought a lot of Louie, so did Mrs. Brooks who was cooking at the Mud Lake camp. The jobber spent a good part of his time in Louie's kitchen, talking with him or just sitting there. Mrs. Brooks sent over bread, cookies, doughnuts and pies, and if Louie had any eggs, Brooks took them back to the lumbercamp. During these winters while lumbering there, they just about kept Louie.

When the lumber job at Mud Lake was finished, the Brooks went outside and ran a hotel in Speculator. Louie missed them, missed the good food given to him by Mrs. Brooks, and missed having Ernest Brooks around the kitchen on the long winter days.

Winter and cold weather and deep snow. Louie got out some pure wool cloth that he had bought by the yard at the Corners to make rag moccasins. He cut and shaped it to his feet sewing several layers together with an extra layer or two on the soles. When he pulled these over his rubbers, his feet were always warm. As he was sitting at the window working on the moccasins he saw three men on snowshoes coming toward the camp.

"Hello," they called. "Anybody home?"

When he saw who they were, he reached for his old friend the Winchester on the pegs over the bunk and went to the door. The three men stood before him. He could see that their packs were light, perhaps empty.

"Are you all right, Louie?" they asked, but their eyes were on the gun.

He knew them. Some of the "Windfall Gang", whose hideaway was in a big windfall near Wellstown. The gang was tough. They were all big men, none under six feet, and had but little respect for the seventh commandment. Louie knew that they did not care whether or not he was all right.

"Va-t-en, toi, toi, oui. Get out. Yo' tink ol' Louie ees ready for die. Yo' lak to fin' ol' Louie so on'y ting yo' do ees steal hees trap, steal hees blanket, hees gun." He shifted the old 38.

"What's th' matter wid you? We come all th' way in to see if you was sick an' if there was anything we could do."

"Ol' Louie no seek. He know hees beezness. Yo' tol' dem ol' Louie ees ver' moche 'live. Dees ol' gun tink sam ting ah do me."

The three quickly started back on the trail toward Mud Lake.

Louie went inside and closed the door. His side was bothering him again. He could hardly get his breath. No longer was he able to take care of himself properly. He had lost most of his teeth and was living on pancakes or on bread soaked in condensed milk and water. He was not as neat at cutting his own hair and gray whiskers, and he would wear whatever clothing the summer sports discarded when they went out. He even looked worse than he felt.

He sat down by the window to recover himself somewhat. "Tomorrow, ah tink ah go on de corners. Ah tink eet do me good, by da holy feesh." And he went to work on the moccasins. When that job was done, he took a gunnysack and what tackle and bait were needed, slipped on his snowshoes and went across the lake where he opened up a few of his old holes in the ice

201

and caught four nice trout to take out with him; for he planned an early start next morning.

In the silent dark of night before dawn he was up and getting into his pants by candlelight. He made tea and after eating pulled his new rag moccasins over his rubbers. With the first sign of grayness in the east, he slung on a small pack of furs and stepped out into the zero air, where he put on his snowshoes and swung off on the trail for the Corners.

Soon the February sun broke through the morning clouds and the long cold blue tree shadows stretched across the snow. There had been a light fall of snow and the shoeing was good as the trail had been broken by the three who had gone over it the day before although Louie's stride was shorter and his swing was a little stiff. Blue jays noisily warned each other of his coming and a tired weak deer stood in the deep snow only a few feet to one side and watched him pass. He did not get inside again until he reached his Pillsbury Camp where he stayed that night.

On the next morning, cloudy and dark, some of the little hills near Blue Ridge seemed much steeper than usual, "bien, bien a pic,"

202

but he put them behind him. When he struck the road, he took off his snowshoes and in the afternoon reached the top of the big hill overlooking the Corners. Beneath a gray winter sky, he stood breathing heavily, a bit shaky, and from high over the town looked far off over the roofs to the mountains across the snowy lake. The strange weakness finally passed; and he who had always been so tireless, so strong, now impatiently pulled himself erect and tried to send out a long defiant wolf howl to announce his coming as he had done so many times before.

The howl was weak and tame. But adjusting his pack on his back, he said to himself, "Ah tink eet do me good."

"Louie, da boy! Louie, da boy!" With his snowshoes under his arm he strode down Page's hill and went into the bar-room at Brooks' Hotel. He slung his pack to the floor. "Ba cripe," he sighed as he sank into a chair, "Ah was glad for be here."

"Hello Louie."

" 'lo Louie, why you old fishercat you."

Being winter, they were all natives.

"How are the deer winterin', Louie? Not much like the packs you useta bring out."

"I'll go back in with you when you go, Louie."

Louie was tired.

Children peeked at him through the door to the house part and Mrs. Brooks appeared. She touched his arm. "You ought not to have walked way out here," she told him.

"Do me good." He reached into his pack and handed her the bundle of fish.

"Trout! Oh thanks, Louie, they'll taste good. I'm goin' to get you something to eat. I'll call you when it's ready."

"No feesh."

"No, no fish, Louie. No pancakes either."

Louie joined the men at the bar. His friendly squinting eyes went from one to another, men who had known him for over forty years. Soon he was feeling good.

"Ba da holy feesh. Louie, da boy!"

In the evening he was suddenly taken sick. Ernest Brooks and his wife did what they could. Louie was in the house of friends. He was put to bed and the doctor called.

Down at the bar they had their own ideas. "It was eatin' all that raw venison that got him," Pants Lawrence said knowingly. "It went to his kidneys." The others nodded. "Anyhow," said Pants, "looks as if I bought him the last slug of whiskey he'll ever gargle down his throat."

The next day, Saturday, Feb. 28th, 1915, the town was told that French Louie was dead.

The Corners felt it. Louie had belonged to them. "Old Louie's dead," they told one another, in the stables, in the kitchens, on the roads.

Ernest Brooks said he would pay for the casket. "Give him a decent funeral."

The school was closed on the day that the service was held in the little Methodist Church. The children sat in the two front rows of pews; and before the casket was closed, they filed slowly past it and each laid a spray of fragrant green balsam on Louie's body. In the procession to the cemetery, about a third of a mile away, the children held branches of balsam in front of themselves as they walked. The town buried him in the back corner of the little town cemetery. He had gone over the last portage, taken the long, long trail in peaceful sleep.

THE END

The hunting grounds are no longer free and no longer can anyone kill game at will and build his cabin wherever his fancy dictates. Louie and his generation are gone and no one will ever take their place.

"An affectionate dear old fellow." "A wonderful character with the best of principles, who always minded his own business." "The most interesting man in the north country." "A queer fellow, hard to find out anything about." "A destroyer of game." "Harmless as a kitten." "Independent old cus." "As honest as the sunshine." . . . So Louie is remembered by those who knew him.

His name will be legend. Those who were not so fortunate to have known Louie in the flesh will know him in the spirit. His name will be spoken for years to come around the evening campfires.

And now the old man knocks the ashes out of his pipe on the toe of his boot.

He has told his story, the story of Louie and the West Creek.

But wait! The oldtimer gazes into the evening mists. "I remember once, when," he starts, pauses for a few moments and continues, "I guess Old Louie wouldn't want me to tell you that one," and he says no more about it.

The night is peaceful. The punkies aren't biting. The low roar of the creek as it pours through the rotting sluiceways of the old lumberdam does not really break the stillness. The tall black spruce and balsam are silhouetted against the moonlit mist of the stillwater. The opposite shoreline and the woods are veiled in soft mystic light and the moon rides high over the mountains. It is late and time to go.

"Good night, oldtimer!"

"Well, so long."

"So long."

The Utica Daily Press printed the following:

FRENCH LOUIE IS DEAD

WELL KNOWN ADIRONDACK GUIDE DIES

Louie Seymour, aged between 75 and 80 years, and known as "French Louie", died at the Brooks Hotel in Speculator Saturday afternoon about four o'clock. He was making one of his periodical visits to "The Corners" as Speculator is known to those residing in that vicinity, when he was taken ill.

"French Louie" was one of the best known and most popular trappers and guides of the lower Adirondacks. For more than forty years of his lifetime he had been located at or in the vicinity of Speculator. He plied his trade on the West Canada and its tributaries and at Cedar Lakes. He lived alone and for all this long term of years he had made a living by trapping, hunting and guiding. Many sportsmen in Gloversville, Johnstown and Amsterdam will recall "French Louie" especially well while there are scores further removed who have followed the lead of the aged guide who even in his later years was able to tire the best of the younger men whom he guided to the hiding places of the trout or runways of the deer.

Just how old "French Louie" was no one ever knew, nor did any of his associates ever know who his parents were. He was known to be a French Canadian. He was of a diffident nature and not in the habit of talking about himself. Those who knew him well estimated his age at being seventy-four. He went to Lewey Lake in the early 70s from Canada. One season he had traveled with a circus. However, the call of the wild rang louder to "Louie" than did the lure of the "big top." A hunter and woodsman by birth and instinct he forsook the sawdust arena and the crash of the band, forswore the glamor of the circus forever to spend his days in the woods and to live nearer to nature's heart.

206

"FRENCH LOUIE," HERMIT, IS DEAD

HAD - HALF DOZEN HOMES IN DEEP WOODS OF ADIRONDACKS.

Louie Had Gait Like Gorilla and Had No Use for Game Protectors—His Greatest Joy Was Bird Sharp, Who Chased Little Birds.

Gloversville, March 1.—Louis Seymour, better known as "French Louie," died Saturday at Brooks Hotel at Speculator of Bright's disease. "French Louie" was a trapper, guide and hermit, who was known all through the Adirondacks and was known by reputation, at least, to many visitors to the woods.

Louie came from Canada. He traveled a year with a circus and in 1873 went to the woods and has lived there ever since. He had a half dozen camps strung from Speculator to Moose river. He lived at all of them, although he favored the ones in Moose River and West Canada Lake regions.

"Louie" didn't know how old he was, or, if he did, he told different ages at different times. He gave his age between 75 and 80 years. Louie was a short, tough-fibered man with stooped shoulders, long arms and a gait like a gorilla. He had no use for game protectors and carried his gun lightly. But Louie didn't kill all the deer that come his way. A few years ago he had a high fence built around an apple tree at the West Canada Lake camp to keep the deer from browsing the limbs when Louie was sojourning at his home over in Moose River country, or at one of his other camps. Louie said that he could have killed this deer, but it was tame and good company.

Louie told his visitors many tales of the woods. He told of a mother bear which he had captured in a trap early one spring and how he found the bear half eaten up by her starving cubs. He said that in the fall deer migrate in large numbers from the West Canada Creek region, where the snow is always deep, to the Moose river country, where it is not so deep, and Louie migrated with them for much the same reason, for he did some trapping. In the spring he made maple sugar and caught bears in traps after they had come out of their dens.

One of the greatest curiosities which Louie ever saw was a man who chased little birds and looked at them through an opera glass. It was the only circus that Louie had seen since he had left his outfit when a young man. The bird chaser didn't pay much attention to partridges, which might have been of some use, but was intent upon finding little birds which most folks didn't notice. When Louie wanted to tell his guests about a funny man, he recalled the one who hunted little birds and looked at them with a double barrelled glass which brought the feathery things close up. Louie said that when he felt lonesome he used to think of this man and laugh.

The hermit thought city folks were odd and very peculiar, but this fellow was the limit. The bird sharp made a date with Louie one winter and went back to the headwaters of the West Canada Creek to find some of the little birds which laid their eggs in the winter time, the way some of the owls do. Louie and the man found the nests all right and the man was tremendously happy about it. "He couldn't have been happier if he had caught a $30 fisher," said Louie.

The death record at the town clerk's office in Speculator reads:

Louis Seymour died February 28, 1915 age about 84 years.

Occupation—Guide

Birthplace—Ottawa, Canada.

Father and birthplace of father, unknown.

Mother and birthplace of mother, unknown.

ACKNOWLEDGEMENT

I express grateful appreciation to all who have helped me in the compilation of this book, those who knew Louie well and those who loaned me the use of old photographs. Those who knew the life at Barber's on Jocks Lake and those who were part of the lumbering on the old West Creek. Trume Haskell of Barneveld, Jim Sturges and Meade Sturges and Pants Lawrence of Speculator, and old-timers like Ike and Wellington Kenwell, Bill Courtney, Bill Rude and Tim Crowley of Piseco, Bill Wright and Eddie Johnson of Wilmurt, and Rock and Burt Conklin, Frank Groves, Byron Cool and George Wandover about days at Jocks Lake, and guides Jim Wadsworth and Mike Lyons, Sol Carnahan, lumberman, and Trume Brown, lumberjack.

Mrs. Carl L. Earley, Halsey Page, Gretchen M. Fish, Mrs. Jessie Conkling, Henry Hart and Earl Kreuzer and many others for the use of old photos. Gene Dunn of Utica and Charles Tompkins of Syracuse for stories of West Creek life and I am thankful to Wilbur Ralph of Barneveld and Bob Hughes and Leland H. Follett of Amsterdam and Harvey Donaldson of Fultonville, Henry Shepard of Gray and Vurner Pilchard of Wells for stories or old photos. And to Howard J. Cole of Johnstown for old railroad photos, and to Mae E. Straight and Beulah Lawton of Northville for material on old stage coach days.

I know that I have left some out, there were so many, but I acknowledge my indebtedness to each and every one. My associations with them have given me many pleasant recollections and happy memories of time spent with oldtimers have been a continuing delight.

HARVEY L. DUNHAM

208

I heard a good story up to Piseco.

Alvah Dunning the old hermit of Racquette Lake spent his early life around Piseco. He had a brother Henry. One day Henry and his wife were hewing some logs for a new house when Bang a shot came from a nearby hill and a bullet splintered the log right between them.

"Pay no 'tention," Henry said to his wife "That's Alvah. He's just tryin' to scare us".

Burr Sturges, as a boy, was chopping wood one day and chopped off a sizeable piece of his big toe. He shouted out, "I have cut off my toe."

His father came up and inspected the chopped off fragment and remarked, "It will make good mink bait."

ADIRONDACK NOTES

ADIRONDACK NOTES

ADIRONDACK NOTES

ADIRONDACK NOTES

ADIRONDACK NOTES